What People Are Saying about *Threshold Bible Study*

"To know and love Jesus and to follow him, we need to know and love the sacred Scriptures. For many years now, the *Threshold Bible Study* has proven to be a vital tool for Catholics seeking to go deeper in their encounter with Christ."
▪ **Archbishop José H. Gomez**, *Archbishop of Los Angeles*

"*Threshold Bible Study* offers solid scholarship and spiritual depth. It can be counted on for lively individual study and prayer, even while it offers spiritual riches to deepen communal conversation and reflection among the people of God."
▪ **Scott Hahn**, *Founder and President, St. Paul Center for Biblical Theology*

"Stephen Binz provides the church with a tremendous gift and resource in the *Threshold Bible Study*. This great series invites readers into the world of Scripture with insight, wisdom, and accessibility. This series will help you fall in love with the word of God!"
▪ **Daniel P. Horan, OFM**, *Catholic Theological Union, Chicago*

"Stephen J. Binz has a unique talent for helping ordinary folks engage the Bible with deep understanding. Graduates of the Hartford Catholic Biblical School are using his *Threshold Bible Study* throughout Connecticut to bring Scripture more fully into the lives of God's people."
▪ **B.J. Daly Horell**, *Director, Catholic Biblical School, Archdiocese of Hartford*

"*Threshold Bible Study* is by far the best series of short Bible study books available today. I recommend them to all the leaders I help train in the Catholic Bible Institutes of several dioceses. Kudos to Stephen Binz for writing books that are ideal for small-group or individual use."
▪ **Felix Just, SJ**, *Loyola Marymount University, Los Angeles*

"Stephen Binz's *Threshold Bible Study* series gives adults of all ages a very accessible way to 'open wide the Scriptures' as *Dei Verbum* urged. Encountering the word of God together in study groups will allow participants to deepen their faith and encounter their Savior, Jesus."
▪ **Archbishop Joseph E. Kurtz**, *Archbishop of Louisville*

"Though the distance many feel between the word of God and their everyday lives can be overwhelming, it need not be so. *Threshold Bible Study* is a fine blend of the best of biblical scholarship and a realistic sensitivity to the spiritual journey of the believing Christian. I recommend it highly."

Francis J. Moloney, SDB, *Professor, Catholic University of Australia*

"*Threshold Bible Study* is a refreshing approach to enable participants to ponder the Scriptures more deeply. This series provides a practical way for faithful people to get to know the Bible better and to enjoy the fruits of biblical prayer."

Irene Nowell, OSB, *Mount St. Scholastica, Atchison, Kansas*

"*Threshold Bible Study* is appropriately named, for its commentary and study questions bring people to the threshold of the text and invite them in. The questions guide but do not dominate. Stephen Binz's work stands in the tradition of the biblical renewal movement and brings it back to life."

Kathleen M. O'Connor, *Professor Emerita, Columbia Theological Seminary*

"*Threshold Bible Study* takes to heart the summons of the Second Vatican Council—'easy access to sacred Scripture should be provided for all the Christian faithful' (*Dei Verbum*, 22)—by facilitating an encounter with the word of God that is simple, insightful, and engaging. A great resource for the New Evangelization."

Hosffman Ospino, *Professor, Boston College School of Theology and Ministry*

"Stephen J. Binz is a consistently outstanding Catholic educator and communicator whose books on the study and application of Scripture have thoroughly enriched my Christian understanding. In our fast-moving, often confusing times, his ability to help us examine and comprehend the truth through all the noise is especially needed and valuable."

Elizabeth Scalia, *writer and speaker, editor at Aleteia, blogger as The Anchoress*

"*Threshold Bible Study* helpfully introduces the lay reader into the life-enhancing process of *lectio divina*, individually or in a group. This series leads the reader from Bible study to personal prayer, community involvement, and active Christian commitment in the world."

Sandra M. Schneiders, *Professor, Jesuit School of Theology at Santa Clara University*

"Stephen Binz has created an essential resource for the new evangelization rooted in the discipleship process that helps participants to unpack the treasures of the Scriptures in an engaging and accessible manner. *Threshold Bible Study* connects faith learning to faithful living, leading one to a deeper relationship with Christ and his body, the church."

Julianne Stanz, *Director of New Evangelization, Diocese of Green Bay*

THRESHOLD BIBLE STUDY

Proclaiming Christ Crucified

1 Corinthians

Stephen J. Binz

TWENTY-THIRD PUBLICATIONS
twentythirdpublications.com

TWENTY-THIRD PUBLICATIONS
One Montauk Avenue, Suite 200
New London, CT 06320
(860) 437-3012 or (800) 321-0411
www.twentythirdpublications.com

ISBN: 978-1-62785-440-5
Library of Congress Control Number: 2018962309
Printed in the U.S.A.

bayard A division of Bayard, Inc.

Contents

LESSONS 13–18

LESSONS 19–24

LESSONS 25–30

How to Use *Threshold Bible Study*

Threshold Bible Study is a dynamic, informative, inspiring, and life-changing series that helps you learn about Scripture in a whole new way. Each book will help you explore new dimensions of faith and discover deeper insights for your life as a disciple of Jesus.

The threshold is a place of transition. The threshold of God's word invites you to enter that place where God's truth, goodness, and beauty can shine into your life and fill your mind and heart. Through the Holy Spirit, the threshold becomes holy ground, sacred space, and graced time. God can teach you best at the threshold, because God opens your life to his word and fills you with the Spirit of truth.

With *Threshold Bible Study*, each topic or book of the Bible is approached in a thematic way. You will understand and reflect on the biblical texts through overarching themes derived from biblical theology. Through this method, the study of Scripture will impact your life in a unique way and transform you from within.

These books are designed for maximum flexibility. Each study is presented in a workbook format, with sections for reading, reflecting, writing, discussing, and praying. Each *Threshold* book contains thirty lessons, which you can use for your daily study over the course of a month or which can be divided into six lessons per week, providing a group study of six weekly sessions. These studies are ideal for Bible study groups, small Christian communities, adult faith formation, student groups, Sunday school, neighborhood groups, and family reading, as well as for individual learning.

The commentary that follows each biblical passage launches your reflection on that passage and helps you begin to see its significance within the context of your contemporary experience. The questions following the commentary challenge you to understand the passage more fully and apply it to your own life. Space for writing after each question is ideal for personal study and also allows group participants to prepare in advance for the weekly discussion. The prayer helps conclude your study each day by integrating your learning into your relationship with God.

The method of *Threshold Bible Study* is rooted in the ancient tradition of *lectio divina*, whereby studying the Bible becomes a means of deeper intimacy with God and a transformed life. Reading and interpreting the text (*lectio*) is followed by reflective meditation on its message (*meditatio*). This reading and reflecting flows into prayer from the heart (*oratio* and *contemplatio*). In this way, one listens to God through the Scripture and then responds to God in prayer.

This ancient method assures you that Bible study is a matter of both the mind and the heart. It is not just an intellectual exercise to learn more and be able to discuss the Bible with others. It is, more importantly, a transforming experience. Reflecting on God's word, guided by the Holy Spirit, illumines the mind with wisdom and stirs the heart with zeal.

Following the personal Bible study, *Threshold Bible Study* offers ways to extend personal *lectio divina* into a weekly conversation with others. This communal experience will allow participants to enhance their appreciation of the message and build up a spiritual community (*collatio*). The end result will be to increase not only individual faith, but also faithful witness in the context of daily life (*operatio*).

When bringing *Threshold Bible Study* to a church community, try to make every effort to include as many people as possible. Many will want to study on their own; others will want to study with family, a group of friends, or a few work associates; some may want to commit themselves to share insights through a weekly conference call, daily text messaging, or an online social network; and others will want to gather weekly in established small groups.

By encouraging *Threshold Bible Study* and respecting the many ways people desire to make Bible study a regular part of their lives, you will widen the number of people in your church community who study the Bible regularly in whatever way they are able in their busy lives. Simply sign up people at the Sunday services and order bulk quantities for your church. Encourage people to follow the daily study as faithfully as they can. This encouragement can be through Sunday announcements, notices in parish publications, support on the church website, and other creative invitations and motivations.

Through the spiritual disciplines of Scripture reading, study, reflection, conversation, and prayer, *Threshold Bible Study* will help you experience God's grace more abundantly and root your life more deeply in Christ. The risen Jesus said: "Listen! I am standing at the door, knocking; if you hear my voice and open the door, I will come in to you and eat with you, and you with me" (Rev 3:20). Listen to the word of God, open the door, and cross the threshold to an unimaginable dwelling with God!

SUGGESTIONS FOR INDIVIDUAL STUDY

- Make your Bible reading a time of prayer. Ask for God's guidance as you read the Scriptures.
- Try to study daily, or as often as possible according to the circumstances of your life.
- Read the Bible passage carefully, trying to understand both its meaning and its personal application as you read. Some persons find it helpful to read the passage aloud.
- Read the passage in another Bible translation. Each version adds to your understanding of the original text.
- Allow the commentary to help you comprehend and apply the scriptural text. The commentary is only a beginning, not the last word, on the meaning of the passage.
- After reflecting on each question, write out your responses. The very act of writing will help you clarify your thoughts, bring new insights, and amplify your understanding.
- As you reflect on your answers, think about how you can live God's word in the context of your daily life.
- Conclude each daily lesson by reading the prayer and continuing with your own prayer from the heart.
- Make sure your reflections and prayers are matters of both the mind and the heart. A true encounter with God's word is always a transforming experience.
- Choose a word or a phrase from the lesson to carry with you throughout the day as a reminder of your encounter with God's life-changing word.
- For additional insights and affirmation, share your learning experience with at least one other person whom you trust. The ideal way to share learning is in a small group that meets regularly.

SUGGESTIONS FOR GROUP STUDY

- Meet regularly; weekly is ideal. Try to be on time and make attendance a high priority for the sake of the group. The average group meets for about an hour.
- Open each session with a prepared prayer, a song, or a reflection. Find some appropriate way to bring the group from the workaday world into a sacred time of graced sharing.
- If you have not been together before, name tags are very helpful as a group begins to become acquainted with the other group members.
- Spend the first session getting acquainted with one another, reading the Introduction aloud, and discussing the questions that follow.
- Appoint a group facilitator to provide guidance to the discussion. The role of facilitator may rotate among members each week. The facilitator simply keeps the discussion on track; each person shares responsibility for the group. There is no need for the facilitator to be a trained teacher.
- Try to study the six lessons on your own during the week. When you have done your own reflection and written your own answers, you will be better prepared to discuss the six scriptural lessons with the group. If you have not had an opportunity to study the passages during the week, meet with the group anyway to share support and insights.
- Participate in the discussion as much as you are able, offering your thoughts, insights, feelings, and decisions. You learn by sharing with others the fruits of your study.
- Be careful not to dominate the discussion. It is important that everyone in the group be offered an equal opportunity to share the results of their work. Try to link what you say to the comments of others so that the group remains on the topic.
- When discussing your own personal thoughts or feelings, use "I" language. Be as personal and honest as appropriate and be very cautious about giving advice to others.

- Listen attentively to the other members of the group so as to learn from their insights. The words of the Bible affect each person in a different way, so a group provides a wealth of understanding for each member.
- Don't fear silence. Silence in a group is as important as silence in personal study. It allows individuals time to listen to the voice of God's Spirit and the opportunity to form their thoughts before they speak.
- Solicit several responses for each question. The thoughts of different people will build on the answers of others and will lead to deeper insights for all.
- Don't fear controversy. Differences of opinions are a sign of a healthy and honest group. If you cannot resolve an issue, continue on, agreeing to disagree. There is probably some truth in each viewpoint.
- Discuss the questions that seem most important for the group. There is no need to cover all the questions in the group session.
- Realize that some questions about the Bible cannot be resolved, even by experts. Don't get stuck on some issue for which there are no clear answers.
- Whatever is said in the group is said in confidence and should be regarded as such.
- Pray as a group in whatever way feels comfortable. Pray for the members of your group throughout the week.

Schedule for Group Study

Session 1: Introduction Date: ______________________

Session 2: Lessons 1–6 Date: ______________________

Session 3: Lessons 7–12 Date: ______________________

Session 4: Lessons 13–18 Date: ______________________

Session 5: Lessons 19–24 Date: ______________________

Session 6: Lessons 25–30 Date: ______________________

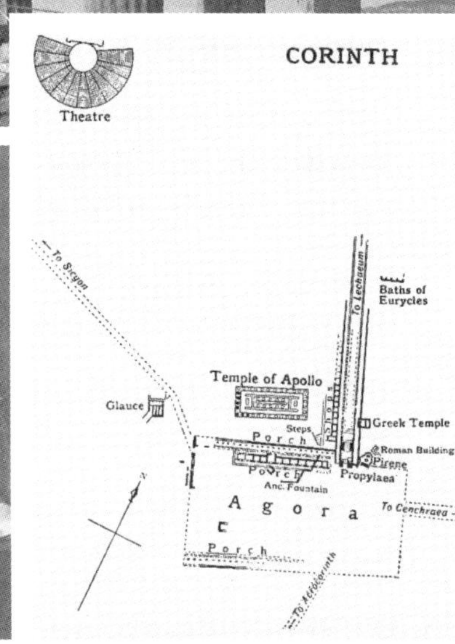
CORINTH
Theatre
To Sicyon
To Lechaeum
Baths of Eurycles
Temple of Apollo
Glauce
Greek Temple
Steps
Porch
Roman Building
Pirene
Porch
Propylaea
Anc. Fountain
Agora
To Cenchraea
Porch
To Acrocorinth
N

The message about the cross is foolishness to those who are perishing, but to us who are being saved it is the power of God.
1 CORINTHIANS 1:18

Proclaiming Christ Crucified

When Paul wrote this letter to the Christian community in Corinth, he was addressing a young church whose members were discerning how to be followers of Jesus in their own unique context. Their faith was rooted in the good news proclaimed by Paul when he founded the church in Corinth a few years before. According to the brief summary of his ministry in Corinth told in the Acts of the Apostles, chapter 18, he had lived among them for a year and a half before moving on to other places. Now, he was writing to encourage them in their struggles as new believers and to address issues concerning the church's identity within its cultural surroundings.

Paul knew that receiving the gospel of Jesus Christ within a pluralistic, pagan world meant undergoing a conversion of the imagination. So, he repeatedly calls his readers to imagine the world and the purpose of their lives in radically new ways. They must learn to envision themselves as the heirs of God's work in ancient Israel, which has come to its completion in the saving death of the Messiah on the cross. They must come to understand how all personal and communal values are transformed by the death and resurrection of Jesus.

For this reason, Paul recalls to his readers that his foundational ministry among them was centered on "Jesus Christ, and him crucified" (2:2). His purpose was solely to give witness to the cross through his words and deeds. In referring to Jesus Christ "crucified" (in the Greek perfect tense), Paul is describing an action completed in the past whose effects continue into the present. Thus, the identity of Christ always remains united with the cross. A living faith in Jesus Christ must always be grounded in a saving relationship with him as the crucified one.

Since this is the way that God has chosen to reveal his truth to the world, Paul determined that he would proclaim the gospel in ways that were consistent with its message of Jesus Christ crucified. The cross cannot be proclaimed with dazzling oratory but only in simplicity and weakness. So, Paul did not preach the gospel in ways that exhibited his own knowledge or eloquence. Rather, the cross molded his style and his entire message. He continually reminds his readers that God works through weakness and that the message of the cross seems foolish in the context of the Corinthian culture.

Paul addresses a Christian community in Corinth whose imaginations were, for the most part, not converted. Their new beliefs appear not to have created a sufficient social and moral realignment of their lives. Their lifestyle remained fully integrated into the pagan Corinthian society, a culture that is inherently antagonistic to the wisdom of the cross. As a result, Paul is seeking throughout this letter to establish firm boundaries between the church and its cultural surroundings, to convert the imaginations of believers to the values of the gospel, and to align their lives with the countercultural message of the cross.

Christians seemed strange to the pagan population because they had no temples, no particular national identity, and no established political ties with the Romans. They met in private homes, greeted each other with a holy kiss, and partook of the body and blood of the one who was crucified in Jerusalem. Paul's preaching that Jesus alone is the Lord confronted the city's cycle of religious festivals and threw into question the performance of sacrifices to the reigning emperor, which was so essential to the cultural life of the city. The overwhelming pressure to conform to the institutions of the city constantly tempted Christian converts to compromise their faith and return to their former pagan practices.

Paul has been away from Corinth long enough for serious problems to arise within the community. As he writes this letter, he knows that the church faces a significant moment of crisis and testing. He also knows that correct living is rooted in correct believing about the significance of the crucified Christ. For this reason, Paul takes up all the difficult issues and reframes them in light of the cross. The crucified Christ is the focus for his discussion of factions within the church, lawsuits, sexual immorality, marriage, meat offered to idols, the Lord's supper, spiritual gifts, and the resurrection.

The gospel of the crucified Christ has tremendous implications for the social structure of the community of Christ's people. As the body of Christ, they are united in him—rich and poor, slave and free—in a network of mutual care and love. Status distinctions are now irrelevant "in the Lord," and all power relations must be reinterpreted in light of the cross. Although the Corinthians had difficulty grasping this vision, Paul knows that submission to the cross will dispel vanity, selfishness, and all the ways that the gospel is being distorted in Corinth.

Reflection and discussion

- How does the gospel of Jesus Christ crucified impact the way that Paul proclaims the gospel?

- What does it mean to say that receiving the gospel means undergoing a conversion of the imagination?

The Setting of Paul's Letter

The city of Corinth was ideally located for the evangelizing mission of Paul. It was situated on a natural land bridge connecting mainland Greece to the north and the peninsula of Peloponnesus to the south. In addition, it had a harbor both to its east and its west, one leading straight to Asia and the other to Italy. The city was, thus, a natural crossroads for travel both by land and by sea. Establishing a Christian community at such a crossroads held the promise of evangelizing all who passed through so that they might bring the good news of Christ back to their own cities and towns.

Although the ancient Greek city of Corinth had a long history, it had been destroyed in a war with the Romans in 146 BC, and most of its inhabitants were either killed or sold as slaves. After lying desolate for over a century, Corinth began to be rebuilt as a Roman colony by Julius Caesar in the year 44 BC. Although the new city was geographically in Greece, it was largely Roman in its architectural design and political organization. As a Roman colony, Corinth was built to cultivate the grandeur of Roman culture and values. Promoting the splendor of classical art, architecture, and religion, the city displayed temples and sculptures dedicated to the imperial family and the Roman gods.

The city was initially populated by freed slaves and Roman military veterans, but over time, Corinth became a lively city where people and cultures of every sort jostled together. As a center for international trade, it attracted people from distant lands, and its population became quite mixed. Although its common tongue was Greek, many other languages could be heard on the streets as well. Like most large cities of the time, Corinth also included a sizable Jewish population. The city quickly grew in prosperity, and by the time of Paul, it had become the largest and most dazzling of the cities of Greece.

In addition to its prosperous trade, Corinth hosted the Isthmian games, an athletic festival second only to the Olympic games in importance. This event, held once every two years, attracted large crowds and generated significant revenue for the city. Most probably Paul took advantage of this occasion to preach the gospel and introduce visitors to Jesus Christ. Evidence of this can be seen in the ways in which Paul uses images of athletic competition in his letter to refer to the Christian life. He urges the Corinthians to be serious about their mission, like athletes training for the race. As athletes train and contend for a perishable wreath, Christians seek the imperishable prize (9:25).

Because Corinth was a city of such diverse population, the church that Paul established there was a mixed, cosmopolitan community. The church was also marked by great diversity in wealth and social standing. The majority of its Christians seem to have been people of modest means and some of them were slaves. Yet, the church also included members who were wealthy and held positions of power. Several owned houses large enough to hold sizable gatherings for the community.

These differences within the Christian community help us understand some of the conflicts that afflicted the church in Corinth. Although they had become Christians, they had not stopped being Corinthians. With its mixed population of Roman freedmen, indigenous Greeks, and immigrants from far and wide, the city displayed a blatant divide between the wealthy and the poor. Desire for individual honor and social standing among the influential resisted Paul's attempts to establish a community based on selfless generosity and the dignity of every individual. There was a lot about the gospel that the Corinthians had not yet grasped, and there was a lot about them that the gospel had not yet changed.

Although Paul came to Corinth in fear and trembling (2:3), he was willing to trust in the power of the cross and bring the good news to this daunting city. In fact, he proudly describes himself as the "father" of the church in Corinth (4:15). The letter demonstrates his resolve to nurture the community in the gospel. And, by the grace of God and the courage of Paul, the gospel of Jesus Christ took firm root there.

Reflection and discussion

- What would have been some of the biggest obstacles to the gospel in Corinth?

- What are some similarities between Paul's context in first-century Corinth and the twenty-first-century context of my life?

The Challenges of Interpreting Paul's Letter

Paul's letter is the continuation of an ongoing conversation between Paul and the church in Corinth. The letter serves as his substitute presence. He had written at least one previous letter to them (which has been lost) and is trying to keep up a long-distance relationship through this ancient means of communication.

It seems that Paul's letter had been prompted by at least two pieces of information he had received. First, he had received reports from "Chloe's people" (1:11). From these Paul learned about some of the divisiveness within the community and the quarrels breaking out among them. And second, he had received a letter from a delegation of Corinthians (7:1). The letter must have contained queries about several issues, and from Paul's answers we can discern those topics that most demanded Paul's attention. Paul's reply, which we call today First Corinthians, is essentially his response to a wide variety of issues and problems raised by these two sources.

Because Paul's letter is a piece of correspondence, we must realize that we are reading someone else's mail. As we eavesdrop on this conversation, we should be clear that Paul did not intend to develop a timeless, theological essay. Rather, he is offering pastoral instruction for a particular community that encountered a specific set of challenges in the middle of the first century. As we read the letter, we are given a privileged glimpse of one particularly difficult moment in the life of the first generation of Christianity.

Because we are reading the mail of the Corinthians and are unaware of many details about which Paul is writing, there is much in the letter that is not obvious to us. The particular problems addressed by Paul are far away and long ago. So, we should not be surprised to find it difficult at times to follow the thread of Paul's thought. But the puzzles should not distract us from the parts that are clear. Paul addresses plenty of issues that have parallels for the church today and that give us plenty of food for thought and reflection.

Because this letter was preserved and widely circulated in the early church, it has become a part of the New Testament canon. God has chosen to offer timeless guidance to his church through this time-bound piece of correspondence. In order to discern God's truth in Paul's letter today, we must first of all step back from the text, distancing ourselves from its ancient context and faraway setting. We must understand its foreignness and confess that it does not speak to our twenty-first-century challenges directly. But then we must draw near to the text again, projecting ourselves imaginatively into the long-ago life of Corinth and learning to see our own lives in challenging new ways. We then listen expectantly for God's timeless truth found in the overlap between then and now.

The Holy Spirit who inspired Paul as he wrote this letter continues to move in the faithful communities who continue to read it. Both Paul's preaching and his letter writing serve as vehicles of the revelation of God. Both are humble instruments used by God's Spirit to teach the church, moving those called by God beyond themselves and into the vulnerability of life lived for God and for others. This divine Spirit is the means by which the word of God comes to the church today through 1 Corinthians.

Reflection and discussion

- What are the inherent problems of understanding when reading someone else's mail?

- What transition do I need to make so that Paul's mail to the first-century Corinthians becomes God's word addressed to me?

Reading Paul's Letter to the Corinthians

Deep insight and pastoral sensitivity make this letter one of Paul's greatest achievements. The work provides testimony from the first century to the difficulties that accompanied the planting of the gospel of Jesus Christ in a pagan environment. Throughout the letter we see evidence of this nascent community struggling with its identity, character, and behavior.

Paul writes to the Corinthians from the perspective of his understanding of what God has accomplished in the world. At its heart is the truth about humanity's desperate situation and the saving work God has accomplished in Christ. This is no superficial self-help message. Paul has come "proclaiming the mystery of God" (2:1). This mystery, planned by God from eternity but hidden from the world, is now revealed by God in this time of fulfillment.

This divine purpose for the world is too profound to be discovered by human insight. It is truth that must be revealed by God because it transcends worldly wisdom. The heart of this mystery, the salvation offered to the world in Christ crucified, is particularly impenetrable to those who pride themselves on their own status and power, for it shows them to be only an illusion. This truth is revealed, rather, to the humble, to anyone who chooses to submit to it. Only by receiving God's revelation with such trust can the depths of God's grace be fully grasped.

Paul knew that he and his hearers were living in a critical time. Through the crucified Messiah, God has intervened to overthrow the present evil order of the world and usher in the fullness of God's reign. The church is living now at that crucial juncture: "the present form of this world is passing away" (7:31), and God's sovereignty has begun. God is now calling this new community, in Corinth and throughout the world, to live a transformed existence made possible through the outpouring of the Spirit and its gifts.

As Paul moves from topic to topic in this letter, he brings this understanding of what God has done in Christ to bear on his responses to the community. How should these Corinthians, poised between the saving event of Christ's cross and the promise of future glory, live in the present? Paul unfolds his answer in these chapters, a reply that remains as challenging today as it was for his first-century readers.

Reflection and discussion

- What is the unique perspective that Paul brings to his response to the pastoral issues that face the church in Corinth?

- What aspects of my own context today make me more open and eager to read this letter?

Prayer

Lord God, you called your apostle Paul to proclaim your gospel and establish your church in Corinth. Prepare my mind and heart to receive these inspired words of Paul as I read his First Letter to the Corinthians. Show me how to meditate on these words each day so that they lead me to prayer. Through the work of the Holy Spirit, stir up in me a desire to respond to these words and allow them to transform my life. Keep me faithful during these weeks to the challenges of study and prayer that your word offers to me.

SUGGESTIONS FOR FACILITATORS, GROUP SESSION 1

1. If the group is meeting for the first time, or if there are newcomers joining the group, it is helpful to provide nametags.

2. Distribute the books to the members of the group.

3. You may want to ask the participants to introduce themselves and tell the group a bit about themselves.

4. Ask one or more of these introductory questions:
    - What drew you to join this group?
    - What is your biggest fear in beginning this Bible study?
    - How is beginning this study like a "threshold" for you?

5. You may want to pray this prayer as a group:
   Come upon us, Holy Spirit, to enlighten and guide us as we begin this study of Paul's First Letter to the Corinthians. You inspired the authors of Scripture to reveal your presence throughout the history of salvation. This inspired word has the power to convert our hearts and change our lives. Fill our hearts with desire, trust, and confidence as you shine the light of your truth within us. Motivate us to read the Scriptures, and give us a deeper love for God's word each day. Bless us during this session and throughout the coming week with the fire of your love.

6. Read the Introduction aloud, pausing at each question for discussion. Group members may wish to write the insights of the group as each question is discussed. Encourage several members of the group to respond to each question.

7. Don't feel compelled to finish the complete Introduction during the session. It is better to allow sufficient time to talk about the questions raised than to rush to the end. Group members may read any remaining sections on their own after the group meeting.

8. Instruct group members to read the first six lessons on their own during the six days before the next group meeting. They should write out their own answers to the questions as preparation for next week's group discussion.

9. Fill in the date for each group meeting under "Schedule for Group Study."

10. Conclude by praying aloud together the prayer at the end of the Introduction.

LESSON 1 SESSION 2

Now I appeal to you, brothers and sisters, by the name of our Lord Jesus Christ, that all of you be in agreement and that there be no divisions among you, but that you be united in the same mind and the same purpose. 1 CORINTHIANS 1:10

Paul Addresses the Church of God in Corinth

1 CORINTHIANS 1:1–17 *[1]Paul, called to be an apostle of Christ Jesus by the will of God, and our brother Sosthenes,*

[2]To the church of God that is in Corinth, to those who are sanctified in Christ Jesus, called to be saints, together with all those who in every place call on the name of our Lord Jesus Christ, both their Lord and ours:

[3]Grace to you and peace from God our Father and the Lord Jesus Christ.

[4]I give thanks to my God always for you because of the grace of God that has been given you in Christ Jesus, [5]for in every way you have been enriched in him, in speech and knowledge of every kind—[6]just as the testimony of Christ has been strengthened among you—[7]so that you are not lacking in any spiritual gift as you wait for the revealing of our Lord Jesus Christ. [8]He will also strengthen you to the end, so that you may be blameless on the day of our Lord Jesus Christ. [9]God is faithful; by him you were called into the fellowship of his Son, Jesus Christ our Lord.

[10]Now I appeal to you, brothers and sisters, by the name of our Lord Jesus Christ, that all of you be in agreement and that there be no divisions among you, but that you be united in the same mind and the same purpose. [11]For it has been reported to me by Chloe's people that there are quarrels among you, my brothers

and sisters. [12]*What I mean is that each of you says, "I belong to Paul," or "I belong*
to Apollos," or "I belong to Cephas," or "I belong to Christ." [13]*Has Christ been*
divided? Was Paul crucified for you? Or were you baptized in the name of Paul?
[14]*I thank God that I baptized none of you except Crispus and Gaius,* [15]*so that no*
one can say that you were baptized in my name. [16]*(I did baptize also the household*
of Stephanas; beyond that, I do not know whether I baptized anyone else.) [17]*For*
Christ did not send me to baptize but to proclaim the gospel, and not with eloquent
wisdom, so that the cross of Christ might not be emptied of its power.

Paul's introduction of himself to his recipients as "an apostle of Jesus Christ" defines what Paul does as a result of God's call. He is "one who is sent out" on behalf of Christ and under his authority. The phrase specifies that Paul did not choose his ministry as a promising career path nor was he selected by human authorities. Rather, he received a missionary charge to bring the gospel to the Corinthians and to countless others through an outpouring of God's grace. As in most of his letters, Paul introduces himself with a coworker, indicating that he sees his apostolic work as part of a ministry team. His mention of Sosthenes recalls that a synagogue official by the same name was beaten by a crowd in Corinth because the proconsul refused to bring charges against Paul (Acts 18:17). If this is the same person, he has become a Christian and a coworker with Paul.

In addressing "the church of God that is in Corinth," Paul makes it clear that the recipients of his letter are not ordinary people but, rather, a consecrated community (verse 2). They have been called by God and set apart as God's people in Corinth. They belong to God and confess Jesus Christ as Lord. As such they are "called to be saints," embodying values that are radically different from those of their surrounding culture. They have been given a unique identity and a clear purpose for their lives, set apart from a confused and perishing world. Together they make up a holy people—they are not free agents, lone heroes of sanctity. They share obligations to one another as well as to God. They are united with sanctified communities stretching throughout the Mediterranean world, all of whom acknowledge the sovereignty of Jesus Christ throughout the earth.

To this particular manifestation of the worldwide church, Paul offers "grace" and "peace" (verse 3). This Christian greeting, common to all of Paul's letters, also demonstrates the church's timeless unity. "Grace" is a Greek greeting, and "peace" (*shalom*, in Hebrew) is a Jewish greeting. Together they express the unity of Gentile and Jew in the worldwide church. In addition, "grace" is the source of the Christian life and "peace" is the full experience of that life. God's comprehensive work extends from its initiation in the lives of believers to its completion, from the spark of grace to the fullness of peace.

Following the salutation (verses 1–3), Paul's expression of thanksgiving (verses 4–9) does not praise the community itself, as he does in some of his other letters. Rather, he gives thanks for what God has done, is doing, and will do among them through Christ. He focuses on how "the grace of God" has been at work in the lives of the Corinthian believers, interpreting their present situation in light of God's promises for their future. They have been given an abundance of spiritual gifts, enriched in speech and knowledge, each gift designed for the upbuilding of the community. But the goal of their life as a consecrated community still lies in the future: "the revealing of our Lord Jesus Christ" (verse 7), "the day of our Lord Jesus Christ" (verse 8). That future time, when the king reclaims his kingdom, will be a day of judgment on the earth. Yet, those committed to Christ will be strengthened to the end so that they may stand blameless before God. The past, present, and future of the Christian life is utterly dependent on the fact that "God is faithful" (verse 9). What God has established, through the "fellowship" of the Corinthian community in Christ, will play its part in the grand drama of God's salvation of the world, from its early beginnings until its full completion.

After Paul's salutation and thanksgiving, he leads into the heart of his letter, appealing for unity within the community and an end to divisions (verse 10). This call to unity aims at eliminating the kinds of factions that hinder the church and impede its mission. He does not seek to impose uniformity on the church, but rather to prevent a tear in the seamless garment of the gospel as it is lived in Corinth. As Paul characterizes some of the divisions in the community—"I belong to" so-and-so—he is surely using sarcasm as he attempts to shock the Corinthians out of their boastful comparisons concerning their status in the church (verse 12). He wants to show that exclusive allegiance to human teachers, boasting, jealousy, and rivalry are childish expressions of individualism—symptoms of an "I" disease within the body of Christ. All such expressions of self-centeredness and self-assertion hamper God's work of creating a cross-centered community.

Reflection and discussion

- How does Paul's greeting of "grace" and "peace" express his desires for the church?

- What impact does the future coming of Christ, "the day of our Lord," make in my everyday Christian life?

- In what ways do envy, jealousy, and rivalry within communities of faith "empty" the power of Christ's cross?

Prayer

Lord Jesus Christ, who has called me to a life of holiness through the grace that strengthens me, enrich my life with spiritual gifts. Help me realize that I have been set apart with clear purpose and certain obligations to you and to your church.

LESSON 2 SESSION 2

For Jews demand signs and Greeks desire wisdom, but we proclaim Christ crucified, a stumbling block to Jews and foolishness to Gentiles, but to those who are the called, both Jews and Greeks, Christ the power of God and the wisdom of God. 1 CORINTHIANS 1:22–24

The Foolish Wisdom of the Cross

1 CORINTHIANS 1:18–31 18*For the message about the cross is foolishness to*
those who are perishing, but to us who are being saved it is the power of God. 19*For*
it is written,

> *"I will destroy the wisdom of the wise,*
> *and the discernment of the discerning I will thwart."*

20*Where is the one who is wise? Where is the scribe? Where is the debater of this*
age? Has not God made foolish the wisdom of the world? 21*For since, in the wisdom*
of God, the world did not know God through wisdom, God decided, through the
foolishness of our proclamation, to save those who believe. 22*For Jews demand signs*
and Greeks desire wisdom, 23*but we proclaim Christ crucified, a stumbling block*
to Jews and foolishness to Gentiles, 24*but to those who are the called, both Jews and*
Greeks, Christ the power of God and the wisdom of God. 25*For God's foolishness is*
wiser than human wisdom, and God's weakness is stronger than human strength.

26*Consider your own call, brothers and sisters: not many of you were wise by*
human standards, not many were powerful, not many were of noble birth. 27*But*
God chose what is foolish in the world to shame the wise; God chose what is weak in
the world to shame the strong; 28*God chose what is low and despised in the world,*
things that are not, to reduce to nothing things that are, 29*so that no one might boast*

in the presence of God. [30]*He is the source of your life in Christ Jesus, who became for us wisdom from God, and righteousness and sanctification and redemption,* [31]*in order that, as it is written, "Let the one who boasts, boast in the Lord."*

In order to help unify the church in Corinth, Paul now begins an extended reflection on the cross. He states that the gospel, "the message about the cross," strikes most hearers as foolishness, and that those who respond to the gospel are looked upon as foolish by the world. Wherever Paul preached the gospel, everyone who heard it knew that this alleged Messiah had suffered a shockingly cruel and shameful death. In the process of crucifixion, he was rejected by his own people, deserted by his disciples, and apparently unable to save himself. Yet, in preaching the message of the gospel, Paul did not conceal the crucifixion as just an unfortunate occurrence remedied by the glory of the resurrection. Rather, Paul proclaimed "Christ crucified." He knew that the crucifixion and the resurrection belong together for the fullness of "the message about the cross." Although this message seems foolish to many, for those who respond to it in faith, it is truly the saving "power of God" (verse 18).

Paul underscores the authenticity of his words by quoting from Isaiah 29:14. For the prophet, "the wisdom of the wise" referred to the plans of Israel's political and religious leaders who fail to trust God (verse 19). But God's saving plan, in contrast to that of "the wise," allowed Jerusalem to be besieged and defeated before rescuing it. Likewise, God's wisdom in allowing Christ to be crushed and put to death follows this same pattern. To proclaim a crucified man as God's son, the Lord of all and coming judge of the world, seemed like utter madness, and the terrible disgrace of the cross exposed the preacher of this message to disdain. But Paul continued to preach Christ crucified. He knew that the resurrection did not cover over Christ's suffering and death; rather, it revealed the crucifixion as the heart of God's rescue plan for the world.

The "wise," the "scribe," and the "debater" are the experts of the world (verse 20). But worldly wisdom, sophisticated speech, and oratorical eloquence cannot elicit faith in those who hear the gospel. God's truth, revealed in the cross, fails to meet the criteria of the world's elite. Pride, arrogance, and self-importance lead to self-deception and obstruct God's revelation. But the humble, the meek, those considered foolish in the world's eyes, these are most open to the saving truth and power of the gospel. Therefore, those who trust in the divine message about the cross must undergo a radical reversal of human desires and ways of thinking.

Paul knew that it was not his task to create a convincing message with decisive logic and persuasive rhetoric. As an apostle, he simply announced what God had done in Christ, making sure that people listened and understood. People's acceptance of the message as divine truth depends on the power of grace and the interior working of the Holy Spirit. The power of the gospel transforms the cross from a mark of terror and domination into a symbol of the power of God's saving love. Only the message about the cross can defeat evil, overcome human arrogance, transform lives, and accomplish salvation.

If the cross is indeed God's means of bringing salvation to the world, then all human standards of evaluation are overturned. The gospel shocks Jews and Greeks alike, who quite understandably seek evidence that is more impressive and proof that is irrefutable (verse 22). Jews, who have been suffering under the world's oppressive powers, seek "signs," like those done by Moses at the time of the exodus, parting the sea and giving food in the desert in order to deliver them from bondage. Greeks, with their tradition of learning and culture, seek "wisdom," like that of a philosopher offering reasonable arguments for lofty truths. So, the gospel of "Christ crucified" is a scandal to Jews and foolishness to non-Jews (verse 23). But for all who are opening their lives to God's grace and the work of the Spirit, who have allowed their values and imaginations to be transformed by the cross, this paradoxical gospel of Christ is "the power of God and the wisdom of God" (verse 24). The saving power of the crucified Christ, called "foolishness" and "weakness" by many, has been shown to surpass all the worldly wisdom and strength that humans can muster (verse 25). With trusting faith, Christians understand that the cross is the saving work of God, disabling human pride, bridging the divide between Jew and Greek, and bringing all people into unity in Christ.

As the cross opposes the values of the world, so too, those called by God indicate that God is not beholden to human standards. The Christian movement brought together people of widely diverse rank and status who acknowledged one another as "brothers and sisters" (verse 26). Paul notes that not many in the church of Corinth were wise, powerful, or wealthy when called by God. Instead, God chose what is foolish, weak, lowly, and despised in the world "so that no one might boast in the presence of God" (verse 29). This pattern of God's saving work in the world follows the same design that God followed in the Old Testament. Paul alludes here to the words of Jeremiah to affirm God's countercultural ways: "Do not let the wise boast in their wisdom, do not let the mighty boast in their might, do not let the wealthy boast in their wealth; but let those who boast boast in this, that they understand and know me, that I am the Lord" (Jeremiah 9:23–24). The history of God's dealings with Israel demonstrates that God, not human merit, is the reason for their blessings. Likewise, God demonstrates to the Corinthians that God alone is the source of their wisdom, righteousness, sanctification, and redemption through the cross of Jesus Christ.

Reflection and discussion

- Who are those filled with worldly wisdom, sophisticated speech, and oratorical eloquence today? Why are they sometimes unable to communicate the gospel to our world?

- How do I see God using the foolish, weak, lowly, and despised of the world to build his church today?

Prayer

Crucified Christ, who is the world's salvation, help me to understand how your cross manifests the power and the wisdom of God. Whenever I grow proud or disdainful of others, turn my eyes to you and show me the way of the cross.

LESSON 3 SESSION 2

Now we have received not the spirit of the world, but the Spirit that is from God, so that we may understand the gifts bestowed on us by God. 1 CORINTHIANS 2:12

The Spirit's Revelation of God's Wisdom

1 CORINTHIANS 2:1–16 1*When I came to you, brothers and sisters, I did not*
come proclaiming the mystery of God to you in lofty words or wisdom. 2*For I*
decided to know nothing among you except Jesus Christ, and him crucified. 3*And*
I came to you in weakness and in fear and in much trembling. 4*My speech and my*
proclamation were not with plausible words of wisdom, but with a demonstration
of the Spirit and of power, 5*so that your faith might rest not on human wisdom but*
on the power of God.

6*Yet among the mature we do speak wisdom, though it is not a wisdom of this*
age or of the rulers of this age, who are doomed to perish. 7*But we speak God's*
wisdom, secret and hidden, which God decreed before the ages for our glory. 8*None*
of the rulers of this age understood this; for if they had, they would not have cruci-
fied the Lord of glory. 9*But, as it is written,*

"What no eye has seen, nor ear heard,
nor the human heart conceived,
what God has prepared for those who love him"—

10*these things God has revealed to us through the Spirit; for the Spirit searches*
everything, even the depths of God. 11*For what human being knows what is truly*
human except the human spirit that is within? So also no one comprehends what
is truly God's except the Spirit of God. 12*Now we have received not the spirit of*

the world, but the Spirit that is from God, so that we may understand the gifts bestowed on us by God. [13]*And we speak of these things in words not taught by human wisdom but taught by the Spirit, interpreting spiritual things to those who are spiritual.*

[14]*Those who are unspiritual do not receive the gifts of God's Spirit, for they are foolishness to them, and they are unable to understand them because they are spiritually discerned.* [15]*Those who are spiritual discern all things, and they are themselves subject to no one else's scrutiny.* [16]*"For who has known the mind of the Lord so as to instruct him?" But we have the mind of Christ.*

Remembering his early missionary efforts among the Corinthians, Paul recalls how he preached the gospel in a manner that befit the message. He came among them "in weakness and in fear and in much trembling" (verse 3). From a worldly point of view, he should have been a miserable failure. He used no lofty speech or manipulative power. Rather, he proclaimed Christ crucified, the eternal truth of God's wisdom condensed in the cross. Instead of exploiting the message to headline himself, Paul offered humble speech and unpolished delivery. In this way he allowed the reality of God's power alone to work through him and bring the Corinthians to the experience of salvation. Thus, the Corinthians can know that their faith is not the result of human cleverness but of God's grace working through the Spirit.

Although Paul rejects "human wisdom" and the "wisdom of this age," he insists that the gospel reveals a divine wisdom addressed to "the mature" (verse 6). Clearly Paul does not refer here to a more sophisticated instruction for the gifted few. God's wisdom is nothing more than what Paul has been discussing all along: "the message about the cross" (1:18), "Jesus Christ and him crucified" (2:2). But among those receiving this wisdom, there are those who are "mature" and those who are "infants" in Christ (3:1).

With this distinction, Paul acknowledges that gradations exist among Christians, ranging from spiritual infancy to maturity. Infants seem to be those who have received the gospel but have not yet incarnated the cross, harboring jealousy and stoking rivalries within the community. The mature are those who have opened their lives more fully to God's Spirit and are better able to understand the status-shattering implications of the cross. Unlike the wisdom of this age, which creates a stratified society of elites and inferiors, God's wisdom nurtures the solidarity of believers, a community standing together under the cross.

Paul describes the divine wisdom that he preaches as "secret and hidden" (verse 7). This does not mean that it is some esoteric teaching that humans cannot fathom. Rather, it means that God's saving plan has been concealed up to the present era because the time of fulfillment had not yet come. However, Paul insists that God's plan of salvation through the cross is not plan B, a change of plans when Israel failed. Instead, it was "decreed before the ages for our glory." Because it was God's design from the beginning, those who are mature can read the Scriptures and understand how the cross of Christ brings God's plan for the world's salvation to its climax.

Humans are incapable of discovering God's wisdom on their own, and for those who refuse to hear, it remains veiled. "The rulers of this age," those who wield power in the world, find the cross incomprehensible (verses 6, 8). In fact, those rulers were so clueless about God's wisdom that they "crucified the Lord of glory." But those who are open to hear, who hope in Christ, are destined to share in his glory. This experience of salvation, what human beings cannot imagine, is our destiny in Christ (verse 9).

While we wait in hope for "what God has prepared," we can begin even now, through "the Spirit that is from God," to experience these "gifts bestowed on us by God" (verses 10–12). The human spirit can know the hidden thoughts and desires of a human being, but only the Holy Spirit can comprehend the mind and heart of God. We have received this Spirit, and thus we can be taught by the Spirit and come to understand spiritual things (verse 13).

These gifts that we have been given by God's Spirit, the ability to discern spiritual things, make us mature enough to understand God's hidden wisdom (verses 14–15). If we allow the Holy Spirit to continue shaping our thinking and forming our values, then we will think and act in the same way Christ thought and acted. We will become the answer to Paul's scriptural quote, "Who has known the mind of the Lord?" because we will, in fact, "have the mind of Christ" (verse 16). This means humbling ourselves, sacrificing for others, embodying the crucified Christ, living a life shaped by the cross.

Reflection and discussion

- In what ways does the preaching of Paul befit the gospel that he proclaims?

- How am I growing from an infant in Christ to a mature follower sharing in "the mind of Christ"?

- Why does a person who has received "the gifts of God's Spirit" have a privileged understanding of reality?

Prayer

Merciful God, no one has seen or heard or even imagined what you have prepared for those who love you. Enlighten me with your Spirit so that I may have the mind of Christ, thinking as he would think and choosing as he would choose.

LESSON 4 SESSION 2

I planted, Apollos watered, but God gave the growth. So neither the one who plants nor the one who waters is anything, but only God who gives the growth.

1 CORINTHIANS 3:6–7

You Are God's Field and God's Building

1 CORINTHIANS 3:1–15 [1]*And so, brothers and sisters, I could not speak to you*
as spiritual people, but rather as people of the flesh, as infants in Christ. [2]*I fed you*
with milk, not solid food, for you were not ready for solid food. Even now you are
still not ready, [3]*for you are still of the flesh. For as long as there is jealousy and*
quarreling among you, are you not of the flesh, and behaving according to human
inclinations? [4]*For when one says, "I belong to Paul," and another, "I belong to*
Apollos," are you not merely human?

[5]*What then is Apollos? What is Paul? Servants through whom you came to*
believe, as the Lord assigned to each. [6]*I planted, Apollos watered, but God gave*
the growth. [7]*So neither the one who plants nor the one who waters is anything, but*
only God who gives the growth. [8]*The one who plants and the one who waters have*
a common purpose, and each will receive wages according to the labor of each. [9]*For*
we are God's servants, working together; you are God's field, God's building.

[10]*According to the grace of God given to me, like a skilled master builder I laid a*
foundation, and someone else is building on it. Each builder must choose with care
how to build on it. [11]*For no one can lay any foundation other than the one that has*
been laid; that foundation is Jesus Christ. [12]*Now if anyone builds on the founda-*
tion with gold, silver, precious stones, wood, hay, straw—[13]*the work of each builder*

will become visible, for the Day will disclose it, because it will be revealed with fire, and the fire will test what sort of work each has done. [14]*If what has been built on the foundation survives, the builder will receive a reward.* [15]*If the work is burned up, the builder will suffer loss; the builder will be saved, but only as through fire.*

Paul continues his analogy of the Christian life as a development from infancy to maturity and as a progression from people of the flesh to people of the Spirit. Recalling again his early missionary work among the Corinthians, Paul says that he was required to speak to them as infants who require milk rather than as mature ones capable of solid food (verses 1–2). But in fact, Paul assesses, they are still not ready for the nourishment of God's wisdom because they demonstrate the childish characteristics of jealousy and quarreling among themselves (verse 3). The spiritual immaturity they demonstrate in creating factions within the community, choosing sides for either Paul or Apollos, are all signs that they are still living as people of the flesh. Self-sufficiency, self-centeredness, self-indulgence—these are indications that the Corinthians are "behaving according to human inclinations." Only a fuller acceptance of the gospel of the crucified Christ will lead them to practice their faith as people of the Spirit.

Paul insists that both he and Apollos are servants of God, each of them carrying on the ministry given to them by God (verse 5). Apollos was a Christian missionary who came to Corinth after Paul's initial evangelization. As a preacher of the gospel, he was skilled in oratory and used his talents for the sake of the church. Clearly Paul sees Apollos as a valued partner in ministry, carrying forward the work that Paul began in Corinth. The fault for the disunity within the community lies in the divisiveness of the Corinthians, not in the character or practice of these early missionaries.

Through two extended metaphors for the church, Paul describes the respective roles that he and Apollos played in the founding and development of the Christian community at Corinth. In the first comparison, Paul describes himself and Apollos as simple field hands given the task of planting and cultivating a crop. Paul, who came to Corinth first, planted the church there, and Apollos, who came later, watered the crop (verse 6). Their work is complementary, but neither of them counts for much because they were simply doing the task assigned to them by God (verse 7). They will receive their wages by God according to what they were told to do, not according to whether or not their work was a success (verse 8). They are powerless to make the seed come to life: it is "only God who gives the growth." God is the unseen, living force who makes the gospel take root and spring up into a living community of faith.

As Paul moves to his second metaphor, he describes the church as God's building and himself as "a skilled master builder" who laid the foundation (verse 10). The church's one and only foundation is Jesus Christ, and Paul laid that firm foundation by preaching the gospel of Christ crucified. Other builders must continue to construct the building upon the foundation, but Paul's warning is clear: "Each builder must choose with care how to build on it." The building materials that Paul asks his hearers to consider—"gold, silver, precious stones, wood, hay, straw"—are ranked from exceptional to inferior quality (verse 12). Those building with worldly wisdom will construct a flimsy house of straw. God's building must not be erected hastily or just for show. It must be constructed solidly from the ground up with materials designed to make the church imperishable.

Since God lets out the contract for the building's construction, he also is the one who inspects the building. On the day of God's judgment, the work of each builder will be assessed. Using the imagery of the prophets—"By fire will the Lord execute judgment" (Isaiah 66:16)—Paul declares that fire will test the quality of each one's work (verse 13). Every person bears responsibility for his or her contribution to God's building. If the building has been erected on the foundation with sturdy materials, the builders will receive a reward (verse 14). If it goes up in smoke, they will suffer loss and discover that they have labored in vain (verse 15). Paul's focus here is the effect of each person's labor on the community, not individual salvation. If the shoddy builders are finally saved by God, it will be as if pulled out of the flames and rubble in the nick of time. Even failures can be saved by God's grace, but they will enter salvation smelling of smoke.

Reflection and discussion

- What are some indications that a Christian community is progressing from spiritual infancy to maturity?

- What is the central role of God in each of Paul's two metaphors: the church as God's field and God's building?

- With God as the owner and inspector of the building, what are some considerations he might use in determining whether the building is constructed up to code?

Prayer

Faithful God, who sent your Son to be the foundation of the church, guide my life so that I will mature in the wisdom of your Spirit. Help me build my life on this solid foundation and contribute to your saving work in the world.

LESSON 5 SESSION 2

If you think that you are wise in this age, you should become fools so that you may become wise. For the wisdom of this world is foolishness with God. 1 CORINTHIANS 3:18–19

God's Temple Filled with God's Spirit

1 CORINTHIANS 3:16–23 16*Do you not know that you are God's temple and that*
God's Spirit dwells in you? 17*If anyone destroys God's temple, God will destroy that*
person. For God's temple is holy, and you are that temple.

18*Do not deceive yourselves. If you think that you are wise in this age, you should*
become fools so that you may become wise. 19*For the wisdom of this world is fool-*
ishness with God. For it is written,

"He catches the wise in their craftiness,"

20*and again,*

"The Lord knows the thoughts of the wise,
that they are futile."

21*So let no one boast about human leaders. For all things are yours,* 22*whether Paul*
or Apollos or Cephas or the world or life or death or the present or the future—all
belong to you, 23*and you belong to Christ, and Christ belongs to God.*

The Corinthian Christians must have felt themselves as rather insignificant, overshadowed by the grand temples to the gods throughout the city. Gathered into their house churches, they experienced none of the pageantry of the great pagan festivals of the city. Yet Paul wants them to be assured that they are "God's temple" and that "God's Spirit" dwells in them (verse 16). Although the Corinthians may have thought first of the many Greek and Roman temples of their city, Paul could have in mind no other structure but the temple in Jerusalem and the Spirit of the God of Israel dwelling there. For Jews like Paul, the Jerusalem temple was understood as the central place of God's presence in the world.

Paul decenters the role of Jerusalem's temple and claims the place of God's dwelling as the community founded on the crucified Christ. God's Spirit can no longer be localized in a sacred building but is to be found in the gathered church. "God's temple," Paul emphasizes, "is holy," and thus it is dedicated to the service of God (verse 17). As the destruction of Jerusalem's temple by the Babylonians was remembered as the great calamity of Israel's history, Paul knows that God will surely deal severely with those who harm or disgrace the church.

If God has chosen to makes his presence known to the world in and through communities of human beings, then the stakes are high. Paul recaps the themes he has emphasized in the first part of his letter, reminding his hearers how to set their thinking right and to recognize the great things God has done among them. They must embrace the seemingly foolish wisdom of God, becoming fools to the world but wise in God's sight (verse 18). For supporting arguments, Paul cites two passages from Scripture. The verse from Job 5:13, "He catches the wise in their craftiness," uses the imagery of hunting to describe how those who present themselves as shrewd to the world get trapped in their own ambition. And the verse from Psalm 94:11, "The Lord knows the thoughts of the wise, that they are futile," emphasizes again the uselessness of human wisdom. Paul has demonstrated that what God does often looks foolish to the world; now he quotes the psalm to show that what the clever think and do looks foolish to God.

Succinctly summarizing his argument, Paul says, "So let no one boast about human leaders" (verse 21). The confidence of Christians lies in the saving work of God alone, not in mere human agents or any form of wisdom found in something other than Christ crucified. Paul again names the three leading apostolic figures for the Corinthians—Paul, Apollos, and Cephas—to place them among all the things God has given them. "For all things are yours," a common expression of the philosophers of the day to affirm human self-sufficiency, is cited by Paul to affirm the complete dependency of Christians on God. Christians do not belong to those who preached the gospel to them, to those who laid the church's foundation, or to those who baptized them. The church belongs to God, and Christ has already defined its mission. It will change and grow in ways impossible to determine beforehand. God has given his people all things, including the world, life, death, the present, and the future (verse 22). All things belong to them only because they belong to Christ and Christ belongs to God.

Reflection and discussion

- In verses 16–17, the three uses of "you" are plural. What difference does this make in the way I understand these words?

- What are some of the thoughts and deeds of the worldly wise that must look rather foolish to God?

Prayer

Lord our God, who has given us all things in Christ, may we become your temple in the world, filled with the Holy Spirit. May we be living witnesses of your presence so that others may come to believe in you.

LESSON 6 SESSION 2

What do you have that you did not receive? And if you received it, why do you boast as if it were not a gift?

1 CORINTHIANS 4:7

The Maligned Ministry of the Apostles

1 CORINTHIANS 4:1–13 [1]*Think of us in this way, as servants of Christ and*
stewards of God's mysteries. [2]*Moreover, it is required of stewards that they be*
found trustworthy. [3]*But with me it is a very small thing that I should be judged*
by you or by any human court. I do not even judge myself. [4]*I am not aware of any-*
thing against myself, but I am not thereby acquitted. It is the Lord who judges me.
[5]*Therefore do not pronounce judgment before the time, before the Lord comes, who*
will bring to light the things now hidden in darkness and will disclose the purposes
of the heart. Then each one will receive commendation from God.

[6]*I have applied all this to Apollos and myself for your benefit, brothers and sis-*
ters, so that you may learn through us the meaning of the saying, "Nothing beyond
what is written," so that none of you will be puffed up in favor of one against
another. [7]*For who sees anything different in you? What do you have that you did*
not receive? And if you received it, why do you boast as if it were not a gift?

[8]*Already you have all you want! Already you have become rich! Quite apart*
from us you have become kings! Indeed, I wish that you had become kings, so that
we might be kings with you! [9]*For I think that God has exhibited us apostles as*
last of all, as though sentenced to death, because we have become a spectacle to the
world, to angels and to mortals. [10]*We are fools for the sake of Christ, but you are*
wise in Christ. We are weak, but you are strong. You are held in honor, but we in

disrepute. [11]*To the present hour we are hungry and thirsty, we are poorly clothed and beaten and homeless,* [12]*and we grow weary from the work of our own hands. When reviled, we bless; when persecuted, we endure;* [13]*when slandered, we speak kindly. We have become like the rubbish of the world, the dregs of all things, to this very day.*

Paul invites the Corinthians to regard himself, Apollos, Cephas, and other ministers of the gospel as "servants of Christ" and "stewards of God's mysteries" (verse 1). In calling these Christian leaders "servants," he is confirming the instructions of Jesus: "Whoever wants to be first must be last of all and servant of all" (Mark 9:35). In the Roman period, a "steward" was the servant who oversaw the operations of a household. As stewards of God's mysteries, the evangelists are charged with distributing God's hidden wisdom, now being revealed through the gospel. Both servants and stewards were under the authority of their master and were accountable to him. As the primary quality sought in a steward is "trustworthiness," so the minister of the gospel must be found faithful to the message of Christ crucified (verse 2).

Because Paul is a servant and steward of Christ alone, he considers it a matter of small significance that he is being judged by anyone except his master (verse 3). He even says that his opinion of himself is irrelevant because no one is in a position to evaluate his trustworthiness. Only the day of Christ's coming, when his light will shine into the darkness and expose the motives of the heart, will provide the sole legitimate and competent tribunal (verse 5). All human evaluations are premature and inconsequential. We must avoid both the despair of assuming failure and the presumption of assuming success in advance of the final judgment of God. On that day, each individual will receive the praise that is due from God, and that is the only praise that matters.

Addressing the community as "brothers and sisters," Paul demonstrates the foolishness of the Corinthians who cause divisiveness in the community, compare leaders to one another, and follow human wisdom rather than the gospel (verse 6). He states how using the example of Apollos and himself benefits the community in two ways. First, understanding the saying,

"Nothing beyond what is written," means that they need only apply to their lives the six Scripture passages he has quoted thus far in the letter (1:19, 1:31, 2:9, 2:16, 3:19; 3:20). Together these quotations limit human pride and call on the Corinthians to trust in God alone. Second, the example of the apostles teaches the Corinthians not to be "puffed up," arrogantly favoring one against another. Paul then punctures their inflated view of themselves with a series of questions: Who? What? Why? (verse 7). It is absurd for them to boast, because everything they have received has come from God's grace.

Finally, in case the community has not been sufficiently chastened, Paul begins to compare the superficial lives of the Corinthians with the apostolic lives of Cephas, Apollos, and himself. While the Corinthians are comfortable, affluent, and even seem to live a royal existence (verse 8), the apostles live conformed to the cross, the only way to Christian maturity (verse 9). Rather than giving the apostles crowns to wear, God has presented them to the world as lowly in status and as prisoners sentenced to death. On account of Christ and united with the cross, the apostles appear to be foolish, weak, and disgraced, whereas the Corinthians appear wise, strong, and honorable in the eyes of the world (verse 10). Describing the tribulations of the apostles, Paul says they are hungry, thirsty, poorly clothed, beaten, homeless, and weary from work (verses 11–12). Yet, despite being scorned and rejected by the world, they respond like Christ did. When reviled, persecuted, and slandered, they respond with blessings, manifest endurance, and express kindness.

Reflection and discussion

- Why are human criteria incapable of judging the faithfulness and trustworthiness of those who labor for the gospel?

- How are Paul's words a sober reminder of the way we are to think about ourselves in relation to the opinions of others?

- How would I respond to Paul's who, what, and why questions in verse 7 to lessen my pride and egoism?

- What are some of the descriptions Paul would use for my own community when comparing it to his description of the apostles?

Prayer

Lord and Savior, who gave yourself in love for the world, show your church the way to conform its existence to the way of your cross. Teach me how to resist the wisdom of the world and to follow the example of Paul and the apostles.

SUGGESTIONS FOR FACILITATORS, GROUP SESSION 2

1. If there are newcomers who were not present for the first group session, introduce them now.

2. You may want to pray this prayer as a group:
   Faithful and merciful God, no one has seen or heard or even imagined what you have prepared for those who love you. Through Jesus your Son, give us the grace of salvation as you teach us how to conform our lives to the way of his cross. Send us your Spirit, so that we may mature in true wisdom, live as your temple, and be living witnesses of your presence in the world. As we study your word given through your apostle Paul, let us be strengthened by the faith of one another as we turn our minds to your promises.

3. Ask one or more of the following questions:
   - What was your biggest challenge in Bible study over this past week?
   - What did you learn about yourself this week?

4. Discuss lessons 1 through 6 together. Assuming that group members have read the Scripture and commentary during the week, there is no need to read it aloud. As you review each lesson, you might want to briefly summarize the Scripture passages of each lesson and ask the group what stands out most clearly from the commentary.

5. Choose one or more of the questions for reflection and discussion from each lesson to talk over as a group. You may want to ask group members which question was most challenging or helpful to them as you review each lesson.

6. Keep the discussion moving, but don't rush the discussion in order to complete more questions. Allow time for the questions that provoke the most discussion.

7. Instruct group members to complete lessons 7 through 12 on their own during the six days before the next group meeting. They should write out their own answers to the questions as preparation for next week's group discussion.

8. Conclude by praying aloud together the prayer at the end of lesson 6, or any other prayer you choose.

LESSON 7 SESSION 3

Indeed, in Christ Jesus I became your father through the gospel. I appeal to you, then, be imitators of me. 1 CORINTHIANS 4:15–16

Paul's Paternal Instructions

1 CORINTHIANS 4:14–21 [14]*I am not writing this to make you ashamed, but
to admonish you as my beloved children.* [15]*For though you might have ten thou-
sand guardians in Christ, you do not have many fathers. Indeed, in Christ Jesus I
became your father through the gospel.* [16]*I appeal to you, then, be imitators of me.*
[17]*For this reason I sent you Timothy, who is my beloved and faithful child in the
Lord, to remind you of my ways in Christ Jesus, as I teach them everywhere in every
church.* [18]*But some of you, thinking that I am not coming to you, have become arro-
gant.* [19]*But I will come to you soon, if the Lord wills, and I will find out not the talk
of these arrogant people but their power.* [20]*For the kingdom of God depends not on
talk but on power.* [21]*What would you prefer? Am I to come to you with a stick, or
with love in a spirit of gentleness?*

Paul explains his motives for writing to the Corinthians—not to demoralize them but to "admonish" them, to teach them a lesson as a father instructs his offspring (verse 14). Using the intimate language of family relationships, Paul addresses the church in Corinth as "my beloved children." Although there are many other leaders who will have influential relationships with the Corinthians, these others are only "guardians," a term in Roman society that designates those slaves charged by the father to escort the children to school and share in their upbringing (verse 15). Although these guardians were vital in the children's rearing, the father played the most critical role in their lives. This is the role Paul claimed for himself: "Indeed, in Christ Jesus I became your father through the gospel." His relationship to the Corinthians is unique because he gave them birth in Christ by being the first to preach the gospel to them.

For this reason, Paul claims for himself a unique connection, a special responsibility, and a distinct authority in relationship to the Corinthians. As their spiritual father, Paul urges the Corinthians, "Be imitators of me" (verse 16). Paul offers his own life as an example to follow in order to teach his children the way they should live. In urging the community to imitate his own life in Christ, Paul calls the church to a mission of active service. Like Paul, they should live sacrificially, offering their own lives to God for the sake of others. As the Corinthians become like Paul, they will become like Christ, conformed to the way of his cross.

Paul has sent his coworker Timothy to the Corinthians in order to help them live according to his example (verse 17). With words of deep affection and praise for Timothy, Paul describes him as "my beloved and faithful child in the Lord." According to the account in Acts, Timothy had already been in Corinth during Paul's original ministry there (Acts 18:5). He is now returning as Paul's representative in order to remind them of Paul's "ways in Christ Jesus." But these "ways" that Paul laid as the foundation of the Corinthians' faith are the same universal ways of Christian life that Paul spread among all the churches he founded. As a faithful child, Timothy has modeled himself on Paul and so he is able to remind the Corinthians of what the Christian life is supposed to look like.

But having already sent Timothy in his place, Paul assures the Corinthians that he himself intends to visit them soon (verse 19). The arrogance that has arisen among some in the community is like that of children who have the house to themselves when the parents have left for a while. Paul warns them that the father is coming home quickly and expects to find things in order. Their pride has led them to much empty talk that is devoid of real power. For true power is found only in God's kingdom, made effective through preaching the gospel and the work of the Spirit (verse 20).

Returning to Paul's metaphor of the father and child, he asks the Corinthians a simple question: "What would you prefer?" (verse 21). As a parent facing rebellious children, he asks whether he should come to them with "a stick" for correction or "with love in a spirit of gentleness." If they continue resisting Paul's authority, he will be forced to administer stern discipline upon his return. If they repent of their divisiveness and pride, he will return with a father's gentle love. He is giving them fair warning and time to get their affairs in order. Much will depend on how they respond to the specific directives that Paul will be giving them in the remainder of the letter.

Reflection and discussion

- What might be some of the characteristics of Paul's life that he invites the Corinthians to follow when he urges them, "Be imitators of me"?

- In what sense does Paul describe himself as the father of the Corinthians? As father to the community, how might Paul find the most helpful balance between discipline and gentleness?

Prayer

Christ Jesus, who sent Paul on his evangelizing mission, show me how to be your disciple. Help me to imitate Paul, offering my life for the sake of others and following in the way of your cross.

LESSON 8 SESSION 3

Do you not know that a little yeast leavens the whole batch of dough? Clean out the old yeast so that you may be a new batch, as you really are unleavened. 1 CORINTHIANS 5:6–7

Warning Against Tolerating Sexual Immorality

1 CORINTHIANS 5:1–13 *[1]It is actually reported that there is sexual immorality among you, and of a kind that is not found even among pagans; for a man is living with his father's wife. [2]And you are arrogant! Should you not rather have mourned, so that he who has done this would have been removed from among you?*

[3]For though absent in body, I am present in spirit; and as if present I have already pronounced judgment [4]in the name of the Lord Jesus on the man who has done such a thing. When you are assembled, and my spirit is present with the power of our Lord Jesus, [5]you are to hand this man over to Satan for the destruction of the flesh, so that his spirit may be saved in the day of the Lord.

[6]Your boasting is not a good thing. Do you not know that a little yeast leavens the whole batch of dough? [7]Clean out the old yeast so that you may be a new batch, as you really are unleavened. For our paschal lamb, Christ, has been sacrificed. [8]Therefore, let us celebrate the festival, not with the old yeast, the yeast of malice and evil, but with the unleavened bread of sincerity and truth.

[9]I wrote to you in my letter not to associate with sexually immoral persons—[10]not at all meaning the immoral of this world, or the greedy and robbers, or idolaters, since you would then need to go out of the world. [11]But now I am writing to you not to associate with anyone who bears the name of brother or sister who is sexually immoral or greedy, or is an idolater, reviler, drunkard, or robber. Do

not even eat with such a one. [12]*For what have I to do with judging those outside? Is it not those who are inside that you are to judge?* [13]*God will judge those outside. "Drive out the wicked person from among you."*

Although Paul's warning that he might come to the unrepentant Corinthians with "a stick" for correction (4:21) might seem a bit severe, the cases that Paul begins to describe make that threat more understandable. As Paul discusses each problem within the community, he is chiefly concerned that the wrongdoing inhibits the church's witness to Christ. Such reprehensible behavior within the community threatens the unity, identity, and mission of the church.

Paul first takes up the case of incest within the Christian community, "a man living with his father's wife" (verse 1). A sexual relationship with a stepmother violates the covenant statutes of Israel—"Cursed be anyone who lies with his father's wife" (Deuteronomy 27:20)—but it was also regarded as a serious infraction "even among pagans." If the standards of sexual morality within the church are no different than in the surrounding culture, then something is badly amiss. The fact that the community has allowed the man to continue the relationship indicates the kind of worldliness that has eroded the church. Paul contends that they should "mourn" in shame rather than be "arrogant" with pride (verse 2). Because the members of the church must be closely bound together, accountable for one another, and profoundly affected by the actions of one another, the offender should have already been expelled from the community.

Although Paul is unable to return to Corinth immediately to deal with this urgent matter, he considers himself to be spiritually present with the church through this letter as it is read in the assembly (verses 3–5). His physical absence does not restrict his responsibility for them and his authority over them as their founding apostle and spiritual father. He has given a severe judgment of this man's sin, and he expects them to confirm that judgment and take decisive action when they next assemble for worship. The disciplinary process is a solemn action of the gathered community invested "with the power of our Lord Jesus" to declare the offender no longer a member of the church in Corinth.

Paul's instruction, "You are to hand this man over to Satan," describes the impact of placing the wrongdoer outside the church (verse 5). No longer inside the domain of God's saving protection, the man is ejected into the destructive powers of the world, which is the realm of Satan. This handing over to Satan is "for the destruction of the flesh," that is, the eradication of the man's sinful orientation. When Paul uses the term "flesh," it does not refer to the fleshly body; rather, it designates the rebellious human nature that is opposed to God. Paul hopes that expelling the culprit from the church might force him to wake up to his sin and repent. The ultimate goal, then, is the man's restoration to the church and his salvation at the time of judgment in the day of the Lord.

Although Paul expresses his concern for the sinner's ultimate destiny, his foremost consideration is the effects of this sin on the community. To express the harmful effects of the offender if left undisciplined, Paul's metaphor refers to the corrupting power of leaven, the part of the previous week's dough that continues to ferment. If this leaven should become bacteria-laden and become a contaminant, just a small amount can infect a whole batch of dough (verse 6). Likewise, the sin of this one man can infect the whole church. Paul extends the metaphor to the Passover festival in which all traces of old leaven are removed from the home and a new batch of dough is baked as unleavened bread (verses 7–8). Since Christ, the new Passover lamb, has been sacrificed, God's people can celebrate with the new Passover bread that sustains and sanctifies them.

When Paul wrote a previous letter insisting that Christians not associate with sexually immoral persons, he did not intend for the church to withdraw from the world into a sanctified ghetto or for Christians to avoid rubbing shoulders with sinners in the course of their daily lives (verses 9–10). What he wanted to say, rather, is that Christians should watch after the internal discipline and integrity of the church. The church must remain a counterculture, giving witness to the world, rather than becoming indistinguishable from the culture around it. Paul urges Christians "not to associate with anyone who bears the name of brother or sister" if that person brings dishonor to the family of God through shameful conduct (verse 11).

God will judge those outside the church, but Christian leaders and believers must keep their own house in order (verses 12–13). Paul's concern is for the church's mission. His command, "Drive out the wicked person from among you," must be evaluated with pastoral wisdom within each community in every age. There is a narrow path between tolerance and intolerance. The former can dilute the ability of the church to witness; the latter can degenerate into self-righteousness and exclusivism.

Reflection and discussion

- Because we are reading mail not directly written to us, there is much information that we are not told. What are some of the details of this scandal about which we can only speculate?

- In what ways do scandals within the church minimize the church's mission to evangelize to an unbelieving world?

- What are the limits beyond which patience and toleration toward another person's sin ceases to be a virtue?

Prayer

Merciful God, who sent your Son into the world to save sinners, keep me from becoming too tolerant or too judgmental. Help me to feel your compassion for sinners without condoning their sin.

LESSON 9 SESSION 3

You were washed, you were sanctified, you were justified in the name of the Lord Jesus Christ and in the Spirit of our God.

1 CORINTHIANS 6:11

Grievances and Lawsuits

1 CORINTHIANS 6:1–11 [1]*When any of you has a grievance against another, do you dare to take it to court before the unrighteous, instead of taking it before the saints?* [2]*Do you not know that the saints will judge the world? And if the world is to be judged by you, are you incompetent to try trivial cases?* [3]*Do you not know that we are to judge angels—to say nothing of ordinary matters?* [4]*If you have ordinary cases, then, do you appoint as judges those who have no standing in the church?* [5]*I say this to your shame. Can it be that there is no one among you wise enough to decide between one believer and another,* [6]*but a believer goes to court against a believer—and before unbelievers at that?*

[7]*In fact, to have lawsuits at all with one another is already a defeat for you. Why not rather be wronged? Why not rather be defrauded?* [8]*But you yourselves wrong and defraud—and believers at that.*

[9]*Do you not know that wrongdoers will not inherit the kingdom of God? Do not be deceived! Fornicators, idolaters, adulterers, male prostitutes, sodomites,* [10]*thieves, the greedy, drunkards, revilers, robbers—none of these will inherit the kingdom of God.* [11]*And this is what some of you used to be. But you were washed, you were sanctified, you were justified in the name of the Lord Jesus Christ and in the Spirit of our God.*

Citing another reason why the worldly wisdom of the surrounding culture is still deeply ingrained in the church at Corinth, Paul comments on the report that Christians are taking legal action in court against other members of the church. He chides believers for their willingness to bring their grievances to be judged by unbelievers and their failure to resolve disputes between themselves. These lawsuits breed factionalism and animosity within the church, and they wreck the credibility of the church's evangelizing mission and witness to Christ.

Evidence indicates that the civil courts were far from impartial and that they were guilty of corruption. The aim of a lawsuit was to prevail over another, often involving an assault on the opponent's character. The courts were biased toward the wealthy and open to bribery. Judges, as members of the privileged class, would give preference to the testimony of their social peers against the testimony of those of lower rank. Litigants of high status could hire professional rhetors to argue their cases and, if needed, to bribe the judges. The lower classes did not have equal access to the courts and were unlikely to win over stacked odds.

Paul points out the fundamental inconsistency between who the Christians are as the church and what they are doing in the world. First and foremost, they are "the saints," the people of God called out of their previous condition of bondage and bound together as a people sharing a glorious future. He draws on biblical imagery to indicate that God's chosen will have a part in the judgment of the world and in ruling it in the age to come. So, if they are to participate in such a destiny, they ought to be able to handle trivial matters of far less consequence (verses 2–3). Paul intends his rhetorical question—"Can it be that there is no one among you wise enough to decide between one believer and another?"—to deflate their arrogance (verse 5). If they were truly who they say they are, believers would not be taking their spiritual brothers and sisters to court.

No matter who wins or loses the lawsuit, it is a defeat for the church (verse 7). The litigious spirit of the Corinthians reveals their self-assertiveness and egotism. If such actions can result in the loss of their identity in Christ, "why not rather be wronged? Why not rather be defrauded?" Refusing to seek redress for a wrong would not only be far better than going to court before nonbelieving judges, it would reveal their understanding and acceptance of the wisdom of the cross. Refusing to "repay anyone evil for evil" and seeking what is noble in the sight of all (Romans 12:17), Paul's advice stands in the tradition of Jesus' ethics of non-retaliation.

The kingdom of God brings with it a radical transformation of values and behavior for believers. Christians sometimes have trouble recognizing that injustice is as serious an offense as incest and other sexual misconduct (verse 10). Moral obligations come as consequences of the Christian's new identity in Christ: "washed," cleansed from their sinful past; "sanctified," set apart for God's service; and "justified," brought into the new covenant (verse 11).

Reflection and discussion

- How does Paul's earlier statement of the Christian way of life—"When reviled, we bless; when persecuted, we endure; when slandered, we speak kindly" (4:12–13)—find a practical example in the advice he offers here?

- Would I rather wrong another or be wronged by another? What if my life were increasingly non-retaliatory?

Prayer

God of justice and mercy, you have called your people from the world and into your church. Give me a love that overcomes resentment and a desire to create unity among the community of your saints.

LESSON 10 SESSION 3

Do you not know that your body is a temple of the Holy Spirit within you, which you have from God, and that you are not your own? 1 CORINTHIANS 6:19

Glorify God in Body and Spirit

1 CORINTHIANS 6:12–20 *12"All things are lawful for me," but not all things are*
beneficial. "All things are lawful for me," but I will not be dominated by anything.
13"Food is meant for the stomach and the stomach for food," and God will destroy
both one and the other. The body is meant not for fornication but for the Lord,
and the Lord for the body. 14And God raised the Lord and will also raise us by his
power. 15Do you not know that your bodies are members of Christ? Should I there-
fore take the members of Christ and make them members of a prostitute? Never!
16Do you not know that whoever is united to a prostitute becomes one body with
her? For it is said, "The two shall be one flesh." 17But anyone united to the Lord
becomes one spirit with him. 18Shun fornication! Every sin that a person commits
is outside the body; but the fornicator sins against the body itself. 19Or do you not
know that your body is a temple of the Holy Spirit within you, which you have
from God, and that you are not your own? 20For you were bought with a price;
therefore, glorify God in your body.

Paul challenges the human wisdom of the Corinthians with an imaginary dialogue in which he first quotes the position of his dialogue partners and then responds to their thinking. He first cites one of their favorite sayings, "All things are lawful for me," expressing their personal freedom to do whatever they want with a clear conscience (verse 12). Of course, this approach to moral behavior could be used to excuse the case of incest, bringing fellow Christians to court, and, in the present discussion, visiting prostitutes, which was virtually unrestricted in Corinth. The men of the community were simply asserting their right to continue participating in a practice that was common within their own culture. In response to their insistence on personal autonomy, Paul insists that Christian freedom does not allow a person to pursue pleasure wherever it leads. Thus, their freedom should direct them toward doing what is "beneficial" to themselves and others and away from doing what will control their lives, so they will "not be dominated by anything."

Next, Paul cites another saying from the human wisdom of the Corinthians, "Food is meant for the stomach and the stomach for food" (verse 13), expressing the natural process of hunger and satisfaction. They were using this argument about food to justify their sexual freedom. If we are hungry, we should eat; if we are desirous of sexual gratification, we should seek it. Paul responds that food and hunger as well as sex and prostitution are all passing realities of this world, soon to be destroyed. What is crucial is the true purpose of the body: "The body is meant not for fornication but for the Lord, and the Lord for the body." So what we do with our bodies in this life is a matter of urgent concern and everlasting significance. The body is not simply a shell to be cast off in the next life, but an essential aspect of our eternal destiny. God has confirmed the importance of our bodies by raising Christ from the dead and has assured us of the redemption of our bodies by his promise to raise our bodies with his same power (verse 14).

Paul follows next with a three-point case against making use of prostitutes, with each of his three arguments beginning with the phrase "do you not know" followed by a reference to the "body." Paul's first question assumes that Christians should understand that the Spirit of the risen Christ is now active within them and that their bodies thereby have been made members of the body of Christ (verse 15). Every relationship in life is affected by this union with Christ. Sexual relations with a prostitute, then, means bringing members of Christ's body and joining them in an unholy union—an unthinkable prospect.

Paul's second argument makes the case that all sexual relations create a one-flesh union (verse 16). Although they may regard their union only as a temporary liaison—he to obtain sexual release and she to secure a living—all sexual acts have enduring consequences. An unholy union with a prostitute violates one's spiritual union with Christ (verse 17). Paul emphatically commands, "Shun fornication!" because no other sin engages the power of bodily communication in so intimate a way (verse 18). What is divinely intended to be a means of sharing one's life with another becomes a momentary coupling for selfish ends. It leaves a legacy of alienation rather than loving intimacy and mutual commitment.

In his third argument, Paul insists that the body of a Christian is "a temple of the Holy Spirit" (verse 19). Because the body is a sacred place of God's presence, we are not free to use it however we wish. We belong to God because Christ has ransomed us from the bondage of sin and death (verse 20). For this reason, our bodily life is meant to give glory to God.

Reflection and discussion

- Consider the difference between the human wisdom of the Corinthians, "All things are lawful for me" (verse 12), and the teachings of Paul, "Glorify God in your body" (verse 21). What is the basic difference between the two views of the human body?

- What are some of the slogans heard today that might be similar to those heard in Corinth? What are their similarities to the sayings quoted by Paul?

- How might Paul's teachings on the sacredness of the body help people today better understand the nature of sexual relations?

- What could I do to follow Paul's exhortation, "Glorify God in your body"?

Prayer

Creator God, who made man and woman in your image, teach me to give you thanks for my body and to know that it is a temple of your Spirit living within me. Show me how to glorify you with all that I think, feel, and do.

LESSON 11 SESSION 3

For the unbelieving husband is made holy through his wife, and the unbelieving wife is made holy through her husband.

1 CORINTHIANS 7:14

Directions Regarding Marriage and Family

1 CORINTHIANS 7:1–24 *[1]Now concerning the matters about which you wrote:*
"It is well for a man not to touch a woman." [2]But because of cases of sexual immo-
rality, each man should have his own wife and each woman her own husband. [3]The
husband should give to his wife her conjugal rights, and likewise the wife to her
husband. [4]For the wife does not have authority over her own body, but the husband
does; likewise the husband does not have authority over his own body, but the wife
does. [5]Do not deprive one another except perhaps by agreement for a set time, to
devote yourselves to prayer, and then come together again, so that Satan may not
tempt you because of your lack of self-control. [6]This I say by way of concession, not
of command. [7]I wish that all were as I myself am. But each has a particular gift
from God, one having one kind and another a different kind.

[8]To the unmarried and the widows I say that it is well for them to remain
unmarried as I am. [9]But if they are not practicing self-control, they should marry.
For it is better to marry than to be aflame with passion.

[10]To the married I give this command—not I but the Lord—that the wife should
not separate from her husband [11](but if she does separate, let her remain unmarried
or else be reconciled to her husband), and that the husband should not divorce his wife.

[12]To the rest I say—I and not the Lord—that if any believer has a wife who is
an unbeliever, and she consents to live with him, he should not divorce her. [13]And if

*any woman has a husband who is an unbeliever, and he consents to live with her,
she should not divorce him. 14For the unbelieving husband is made holy through
his wife, and the unbelieving wife is made holy through her husband. Otherwise,
your children would be unclean, but as it is, they are holy. 15But if the unbelieving
partner separates, let it be so; in such a case the brother or sister is not bound. It
is to peace that God has called you. 16Wife, for all you know, you might save your
husband. Husband, for all you know, you might save your wife.*

*17However that may be, let each of you lead the life that the Lord has assigned, to
which God called you. This is my rule in all the churches. 18Was anyone at the time
of his call already circumcised? Let him not seek to remove the marks of circumci-
sion. Was anyone at the time of his call uncircumcised? Let him not seek circum-
cision. 19Circumcision is nothing, and uncircumcision is nothing; but obeying the
commandments of God is everything. 20Let each of you remain in the condition in
which you were called. 21Were you a slave when called? Do not be concerned about
it. Even if you can gain your freedom, make use of your present condition now more
than ever. 22For whoever was called in the Lord as a slave is a freed person belong-
ing to the Lord, just as whoever was free when called is a slave of Christ. 23You were
bought with a price; do not become slaves of human masters. 24In whatever condi-
tion you were called, brothers and sisters, there remain with God.*

Paul now begins to respond to a variety of issues raised in a letter to him from the Corinthians. He offers advice to the married, unmarried, widowed, and those in other states of life. His teachings demonstrate a remarkable mutuality in the relationships of men and women. Although he urges the Corinthians to remain in whatever state of life they find themselves, he helps them understand how to discern the best way to serve God.

Paul begins by quoting a line from the Corinthian letter that states the position of some in the community: "It is well for a man not to touch a woman" (verse 1). Some in the church apparently believed that ordinary married life was unsuited for their new spiritual identity in Christ. Others found their spouses withdrawing from the sexual relationship or even separating from marriage in the interests of an ascetical lifestyle. Paul's clear and practical response holds that marriage should be the norm, and sexual relations within marriage are natural and necessary (verses 2–3). Husbands should be willing to respond to the sexual desires of the wife and vice versa. Paul describes the dynamics of marital relations in a strikingly reciprocal way. Spouses are neither placed in a hierarchical relation with one over the other nor set apart as autonomous units doing as they please. Each partner has a kind of authority over the other that results in mutual submission (verse 4).

Paul allows for one exception to the general guidelines he has counseled, a "concession" to the desire of some Corinthians to practice sexual abstinence as a spiritual discipline (verses 5–6). He permits it if two conditions are met: first, both spouses must be in agreement, and second, it must be temporary. Paul insists that refraining from sexual union in a marriage is not a necessary path to spiritual growth, although he does allow its limited practice in special circumstances. Although Paul himself is celibate, he teaches that everyone has their own "particular gift [*charisma,* in Greek] from God" (verse 7). We don't know whether Paul was once married or never married, but he understands that the gift of celibacy offers freedom and opportunity for extensive service to God. Yet, he also knows that everyone is responsible and privileged to use whatever gifts God has given for God's own purposes.

After responding to those who are married, Paul addresses the concerns of those who are not currently married, particularly those who have lost a spouse through death (verses 8–9). For these, Paul declares that he believes it is better to remain unmarried. Because of the gospel, there is a new value to the single life, the ability to be more free and flexible to serve God. But Paul again advises that the choice be made in the context of discerning spiritual gifts. "Self-control" is not so much a matter of willpower as it is a fruit of the Spirit (Gal 5:23). Unmarried persons should recognize the gift or its absence as they discern their choices.

Returning to address those who are married, Paul confirms the teaching of Jesus that husbands and wives must not divorce one another (verses 10–11), a stance more stringent than any found in Judaism or Greco-Roman culture. But Paul adds his own advice that if the wife should separate from her husband, she should either remain unmarried or reconcile to her husband. Paul then takes up an issue that the teaching of Jesus did not envision: the marriage of Christians to unbelieving partners (verses 12–13). Although some in Corinth must have thought that a Christian should not share life with one who insists on living in the realm of darkness, Paul counsels that the believer should stay with the unbelieving spouse as long as the unbeliever is willing to maintain the marriage. Christian spouses must not initiate divorce, because they make the union holy, sanctifying both the unbelieving spouse and the children (verse 14). However, if the unbeliever acts to terminate the marriage, then the Christian spouse is no longer bound by the marriage commitment (verse 15). Consistently, Paul states his teachings in a way that applies symmetrically to men and women in the church. Both wives and husbands can be the instruments of God's salvation in the lives of their spouses (verse 16). Through the contagious holiness of the Christian family, God's saving power is at work bringing peace to all.

Continuing to address the concerns of some in Corinth that their life in Christ requires them to alter their present status, Paul consistently urges them to continue living in whatever condition they were called by the Lord (verses 17, 20, 24). For example, those men who were already circumcised before their Christian calling should not seek to have the mark of circumcision removed, nor should the uncircumcised become circumcised (verse 18). What matters is that they live faithfully in the new life they've been given (verse 19). Similarly, whether one was a slave or free when called by Christ is relatively unimportant (verse 21). Because the one who was a slave is now a freed person in Christ, and the one who was a free person has become "a slave of Christ" (verse 22). Both have been "bought with a price": the slaves have been ransomed by Christ into freedom, and the free persons have been purchased into bondage to the Lord who has paid the price (verse 23).

Reflection and discussion

- How does Paul contradict those teaching that Christian spouses should refrain from sexual relations?

- What indicates to me that Paul considers men and women to have equal privileges and responsibilities in marriage and the single life?

- What guidance does Paul offer to me in my own state of life?

- What help does Paul offer for those discerning either marriage or singleness?

Prayer

Lord Jesus, who paid the price to redeem your people, help me to view my daily responsibilities from the perspective of eternity. Give me the grace to discern your will for my life and to remain faithful to your call.

LESSON 12 | SESSION 3

I have no command of the Lord, but I give my opinion as one who by the Lord's mercy is trustworthy. I think that, in view of the impending crisis, it is well for you to remain as you are.

1 CORINTHIANS 7:25–26

Remaining in Your Present State of Life

1 CORINTHIANS 7:25–40 25 *Now concerning virgins, I have no command of the Lord, but I give my opinion as one who by the Lord's mercy is trustworthy.* 26 *I think that, in view of the impending crisis, it is well for you to remain as you are.* 27 *Are you bound to a wife? Do not seek to be free. Are you free from a wife? Do not seek a wife.* 28 *But if you marry, you do not sin, and if a virgin marries, she does not sin. Yet those who marry will experience distress in this life, and I would spare you that.* 29 *I mean, brothers and sisters, the appointed time has grown short; from now on, let even those who have wives be as though they had none,* 30 *and those who mourn as though they were not mourning, and those who rejoice as though they were not rejoicing, and those who buy as though they had no possessions,* 31 *and those who deal with the world as though they had no dealings with it. For the present form of this world is passing away.* 32 *I want you to be free from anxieties. The unmarried man is anxious about the affairs of the Lord, how to please the Lord;* 33 *but the married man is anxious about the affairs of the world, how to please his wife,* 34 *and his interests are divided. And the unmarried woman and the virgin are anxious about the affairs of the Lord, so that they may be holy in body and spirit; but the married woman is anxious about the affairs of the world, how to please her*

husband. [35]*I say this for your own benefit, not to put any restraint upon you, but to*
promote good order and unhindered devotion to the Lord.

[36]*If anyone thinks that he is not behaving properly toward his fiancée, if his*
passions are strong, and so it has to be, let him marry as he wishes; it is no sin. Let
them marry. [37]*But if someone stands firm in his resolve, being under no necessity*
but having his own desire under control, and has determined in his own mind to
keep her as his fiancée, he will do well. [38]*So then, he who marries his fiancée does*
well; and he who refrains from marriage will do better.

[39]*A wife is bound as long as her husband lives. But if the husband dies, she is*
free to marry anyone she wishes, only in the Lord. [40]*But in my judgment she is more*
blessed if she remains as she is. And I think that I too have the Spirit of God.

Paul treats a variety of issues in rapid succession, giving his trustworthy opinion (verse 25). The question raised by the Corinthians is whether young people ought to marry or whether as Christians they are now obliged to remain unmarried. Consistent with his other teachings, Paul counsels that it is better that they remain as they are. But if they choose to marry, there is no wrong in that (verses 26–28). The decision lies with the persons involved, although Paul encourages them to stay unmarried if they are able to choose that course freely and decisively (verse 37). "So then, he who marries his fiancée does well; and he who refrains from marriage will do better" (verse 38).

Paul offers two reasons why unmarried people ought to remain unmarried. In explaining the first reason, Paul states: "Those who marry will experience distress in this life, and I would spare you that" (verse 28). Perhaps Paul is referring to the cares and sorrows of raising a family and the pains and dangers of childbearing. Possibly Paul is speaking out of some sorrowful experience of his own. Paul certainly knows that marriage brings obligations and complications that prevent believers from serving the Lord as unreservedly as they might otherwise. He knows that marriage leads to divided interests: married Christians must consider how to produce a family income, manage a home and children, and please their spouse rather than focusing single-mindedly on a devoted relationship with the Lord (verses 32–35).

Paul's second reason for advising unmarried people to remain unmarried is because "the appointed time has grown short" (verse 29) and "the present form of this world is passing away" (verse 31). Between these two phrases, Paul lists five examples in which this distinctive Christian vision of the world ought to determine how believers live in the present. Regarding marriage, they should remember not to identity their lives with even the dearest of earthly bonds, because only their relationship with the Lord is ultimate. Regarding mourning and rejoicing, they must not be consumed with either, because weeping and laughter are not their final condition. Regarding buying possessions, they must not allow acquisitions to distract themselves from what is truly important or become consumed by their consuming. And regarding dealings with the world, they must not become engaged with the world in such a way as to become enmeshed in it. The world must never be the means whereby Christians attempt to create and define their lives.

Paul is not concerned about the length of time that is left, but about how life in Christ has changed how Christians experience that time. The life we know in Christ has compressed time in such a way that our future salvation can already be experienced in the present. And so, we live in the present with radically altered values as to what matters and what does not. The church is living in that critical juncture in which the former age is passing away and the glorious day of the Lord is arriving. This age of the church is a divinely appointed time marked by the activity of God's Spirit and the evangelizing mission to the world. We must live with a watchful awareness of the coming of the Lord and consider all things in light of his final judgment. This sense of expectation ought to pervade the life of every Christian, enabling us to look to the future with joyful hope, knowing that our successes and failures, our roles and affiliations, and our status in the things of this world mean little in the eternal scheme.

Reflection and discussion

- When is it appropriate to make a change in one's state of life, and when is it not?

- How realistic are Paul's two reasons why he recommends that unmarried people remain unmarried?

- In what way does becoming a Christian change a person's outlook toward the things of the world and the priorities of life?

Prayer

Glorious Lord, who will come again to judge the living and the dead, help me to live in the present in a way that anticipates the glorious future you have promised. Keep me focused on the things of life that last forever.

SUGGESTIONS FOR FACILITATORS, GROUP SESSION 3

1. Welcome group members and ask if there are any announcements anyone would like to make.
2. You may want to pray this prayer as a group:
   Lord Jesus Christ, help us to learn from your apostle Paul how to follow in the way of your cross, to proclaim your gospel to the world, and to give our lives for the sake of others. Give us a love that overcomes resentment, a genuine compassion for sinners, and a desire to create unity within your church. Help us to live our daily responsibilities from the perspective of eternity, always seeking to discern your will for our lives in a way that anticipates the glorious future you have promised.
3. Ask one or more of the following questions:
   - Which thought from the lessons this week stands out most memorably to you?
   - What is the most important lesson you learned through your study this week?
4. Discuss lessons 7 through 12. Choose one or more of the questions for reflection and discussion from each lesson to discuss as a group. You may want to ask group members which question was most challenging or helpful to them as you review each lesson.
5. Remember that there are no definitive answers for these discussion questions. The insights of group members will add to the understanding of all. None of these questions require an expert.
6. After talking about each lesson, instruct group members to complete lessons 13 through 18 on their own during the six days before the next group meeting. They should write out their own answers to the questions as preparation for next week's group discussion.
7. Ask the group if anyone is having any particular problems with the Bible study during the week. You may want to share advice and encouragement within the group.
8. Conclude by praying aloud together the prayer at the end of one of the lessons discussed. You may add to the prayer based on the sharing that has occurred in the group.

**But when you thus sin against members of your family,
and wound their conscience when it is weak,
you sin against Christ.** 1 CORINTHIANS 8:12

Knowledge Puffs Up, but Love Builds Up

1 CORINTHIANS 8:1–13 1*Now concerning food sacrificed to idols: we know that*
"all of us possess knowledge." Knowledge puffs up, but love builds up. 2*Anyone who*
claims to know something does not yet have the necessary knowledge; 3*but anyone*
who loves God is known by him.

4*Hence, as to the eating of food offered to idols, we know that "no idol in the*
world really exists," and that "there is no God but one." 5*Indeed, even though there*
may be so-called gods in heaven or on earth—as in fact there are many gods and
*many lords—*6*yet for us there is one God, the Father, from whom are all things and*
for whom we exist, and one Lord, Jesus Christ, through whom are all things and
through whom we exist.

7*It is not everyone, however, who has this knowledge. Since some have become*
so accustomed to idols until now, they still think of the food they eat as food offered
to an idol; and their conscience, being weak, is defiled. 8*"Food will not bring us*
close to God." We are no worse off if we do not eat, and no better off if we do. 9*But*
take care that this liberty of yours does not somehow become a stumbling block
to the weak. 10*For if others see you, who possess knowledge, eating in the temple*
of an idol, might they not, since their conscience is weak, be encouraged to the
point of eating food sacrificed to idols? 11*So by your knowledge those weak believ-*
ers for whom Christ died are destroyed. 12*But when you thus sin against members*

of your family, and wound their conscience when it is weak, you sin against Christ.
13*Therefore, if food is a cause of their falling, I will never eat meat, so that I may not cause one of them to fall.*

Having addressed issues of sexuality and marriage, Paul abruptly turns to another item brought to his attention by the Corinthians: "Concerning food sacrificed to idols" (verse 1). The question of whether or not Christians could eat food that had been sacrificed to pagan gods was a significant issue in Corinth. Because banquets at pagan temples were important civic functions, some Christians continued to attend them and eat meat that had been sacrificed. Not to do so would have forfeited social connections and advancement. Other Christians were scandalized by this and refused even to buy meat in public markets because such meat was sometimes left over from sacrifices. Although the issue might seem irrelevant to us, the way that Paul dealt with it is certainly pertinent for the church today.

Paul begins his response by quoting from the Corinthians' letter: "All of us possess knowledge." Their knowledge seems to be the objective content of Christian belief used by the Corinthians to rationalize their practice of eating food offered to idols. This "knowledge" included the fact that there is only one God and no other gods really exist; therefore, idols are nothing more than lifeless statues, having no power to help or harm anyone. While not disagreeing with this knowledge, Paul points out the dangers of a prideful use of knowledge alone to determine Christian practice: "Knowledge puffs up, but love builds up." Knowledge can easily be misapplied and is always defective if it fails to build up the community in love. Those who boast in their own knowledge demonstrate that they do not yet have real understanding, "the necessary knowledge" (verse 2). What matters most is God's knowledge of us, a knowledge that leads to our love of God, a knowledge that sets Christians apart from worshipers of other gods (verse 3).

In response to the Corinthians' knowledge of monotheism and their knowledge that "no idol really exists" (verse 4), Paul offers another sense in which "in fact there are many gods and many lords" (verse 5). The fact that people revere what they consider to be gods indicates that there is some reality to these "so-called gods." Even though for Christians there is one God, the Father, and one Lord, Jesus Christ (verse 6), Corinth was teeming with gods that were real rivals to the one God. For whatever people worship is indeed a god for them. A clear choice must be made because consorting with the many other gods and lords disavows the relationship with the one God and one Lord. The Christian confession of faith excludes any participation in idolatry, even if it appears to be meaningless and harmless.

Paul turns to the potential effects of eating food offered to idols on other believers who might not have the intellectual sophistication to rationalize the practice (verse 7). Because most of the Corinthians in Corinth are recent converts from paganism, their former association with the gods is deeply ingrained in their consciousness. Eating sanctified food had always been an act honoring the gods hidden within the idols. Even though some Corinthians have argued that "food will not bring us close to God" (verse 8), Paul will continue to show (especially in chapter 10) that sharing food offered to pagan gods, in fact, can lead to a partnership with demonic powers and destroy the Christian faith of a new believer.

Paul warns his hearers about the consequences their behavior can have on those whose moral compass is weak (verse 9). Such inconsiderate and careless conduct can set a bad example and cause a new believer to revert to idolatry (verse 10). Their misguided "knowledge," used in a self-satisfying way, can lead to spiritual wreckage of the "weak believers for whom Christ died" (verse 11). This destructive wounding of the conscience of another is a "sin" against Christ and against members of the Christian family (verse 12).

Paul concludes with a personal commitment. Given the serious nature of the sin of scandal against fellow Christians, he will avoid anything that might put a weak believer at spiritual risk (verse 13). His commitment shows Christians that they have a serious responsibility toward fellow believers. The common good must always be elevated above any self-interest that could bring harm to others.

Reflection and discussion

- How can I reconcile the truth of the Corinthians, "There is no God but one" (verse 4), and Paul's statement, "In fact there are many gods and many lords" (verse 5)?

- Why does Paul hold that knowledge alone is never sufficient when assessing the needs of a Christian community?

- In what sense is the issue of eating food offered to idols a dispute between individual rights and the common good of the community? What is an example of a similar dispute today?

Prayer

God our Father, from whom are all things and for whom we exist, and Lord Jesus Christ, through whom are all things and through whom we exist, help me admit my selfish desires and respond to the struggles of the people around me.

LESSON 14 | SESSION 4

If I proclaim the gospel, this gives me no ground for boasting, for an obligation is laid on me, and woe to me if I do not proclaim the gospel! 1 CORINTHIANS 9:16

Paul's Work as an Apostle

1 CORINTHIANS 9:1–18 *[1]Am I not free? Am I not an apostle? Have I not seen*
Jesus our Lord? Are you not my work in the Lord? [2]If I am not an apostle to others,
at least I am to you; for you are the seal of my apostleship in the Lord.

[3]This is my defense to those who would examine me. [4]Do we not have the right
to our food and drink? [5]Do we not have the right to be accompanied by a believing
wife, as do the other apostles and the brothers of the Lord and Cephas? [6]Or is it only
Barnabas and I who have no right to refrain from working for a living? [7]Who at
any time pays the expenses for doing military service? Who plants a vineyard and
does not eat any of its fruit? Or who tends a flock and does not get any of its milk?

[8]Do I say this on human authority? Does not the law also say the same? [9]For
it is written in the law of Moses, "You shall not muzzle an ox while it is treading
out the grain." Is it for oxen that God is concerned? [10]Or does he not speak entirely
for our sake? It was indeed written for our sake, for whoever plows should plow in
hope and whoever threshes should thresh in hope of a share in the crop. [11]If we have
sown spiritual good among you, is it too much if we reap your material benefits?
[12]If others share this rightful claim on you, do not we still more?

Nevertheless, we have not made use of this right, but we endure anything rather
than put an obstacle in the way of the gospel of Christ. [13]Do you not know that those
who are employed in the temple service get their food from the temple, and those who
serve at the altar share in what is sacrificed on the altar? [14]In the same way, the Lord
commanded that those who proclaim the gospel should get their living by the gospel.

15 But I have made no use of any of these rights, nor am I writing this so that
they may be applied in my case. Indeed, I would rather die than that—no one will
deprive me of my ground for boasting! 16 If I proclaim the gospel, this gives me no
ground for boasting, for an obligation is laid on me, and woe to me if I do not pro-
claim the gospel! 17 For if I do this of my own will, I have a reward; but if not of my
own will, I am entrusted with a commission. 18 What then is my reward? Just this:
that in my proclamation I may make the gospel free of charge, so as not to make
full use of my rights in the gospel.

While Paul offers fascinating information about his apostolic life and the motivation of his mission, he never strays from his discussion of food sacrificed to idols. He focuses on his own practices as an apostle but only as an example of the attitude he wishes the Corinthians to adopt. While seeming to exalt his freedom and his rights, his intent is to show how he sets aside these personal advantages in order to win others to the gospel of Christ. He wants to show the Corinthians how to voluntarily set aside their right to eat food that honors idols. He hopes that his willingness to sacrifice for others in his missionary service will motivate the Corinthians to give up their personal desires so as to avoid causing others to slip back into idolatry.

Paul begins by declaring his own freedom (verse 1). Yet, Paul wants the Corinthians to understand freedom not according to their slogan, "All things are lawful for me" (6:12), but in a way that directs it to the good of the community. Freed by an appearance of the risen Lord, Paul was sent as an apostle to Corinth. Indeed, they are the "seal" of his apostleship, the authorized attestation of his mission (verse 2).

Paul frames his discussion in the form of a "defense" against anyone who would challenge his freedom and rights (verse 4). His series of rhetorical questions is aimed at affirming his authority as an apostle to receive hospitality and be supported financially by the communities he serves. This includes the right to food and drink as well as the right to take a wife along on the journey who would also receive support from the community (verses 4–5). In contrast to the other apostolic missionaries, Paul refers to himself and Barnabas in a way that indicates that they did not claim or accept financial support, nor did they travel with the companionship of a spouse. Instead, they worked for a living in order to forgo the privileges that others receive (verse 6).

The rhetoric of Paul's case rises as he continues to demonstrate the reasonableness of apostles taking support from the congregations in which they minister. Soldiers, vine growers, and shepherds all receive their livelihood in a way that derives from their work (verse 7). The Torah itself includes God's command that an ox must be allowed to enjoy benefits from its work while threshing grain (Deuteronomy 25:4). If the law insists that animals be permitted to eat from the crops in the fields that they are working, how much more should human laborers have the right to do so (verses 9–10). Applying this biblical application to the rights of apostles, Paul reasons that those who have sown the seeds of the gospel should at least reap some material support for their labor (verse 11). Continuing his case, Paul shows that those in religious service, including the priests and those employed at the temple, receive a share in the offerings (verse 13). And finally, his most important evidence comes from the teaching of Jesus himself, whose instructions when sending out his disciples included the assurance that the laborer is worthy of his wages (verse 14).

Having persuasively established his rights as an apostle to receive support, Paul declares that he has not made use of these rights (verses 12, 15). Why? Because he does not want to "put an obstacle in the way of the gospel of Christ." Potential converts may draw back from the gospel if they imagine they could incur financial obligations by accepting it. Paul wants to avoid any impression that he preaches in order to earn a living. So, Paul lowers his status and works with his hands, perhaps also appealing to the lower classes. But most importantly, Paul gives up his rights for the sake of others out of Christian love. He says he would rather die than live off the gospel. So he refuses to exercise his right to be supported, suffering from weariness and glorying in his weakness. His only "ground for boasting" is what God has done in him and through him by grace. For God has laid an "obligation" on him, and he is compelled to proclaim the gospel (verse 16). Paul can do nothing other than what God has commissioned him to do. The initiative for his apostolic mission comes entirely from God (verse 17). He works not for himself but to bring increase to God. The only reward he desires is no reward at all (verse 18).

This is the example from his ministry that Paul desires to impress on the Corinthians who claim the freedom and rights to dine on food offered to idols.

Although Paul is fully free and has every right, he sets aside his privilege to become a servant of Christ and to sacrifice for the salvation of many. He wants the Corinthians to imitate his self-sacrificing and all-consuming concern for others as something that reveals Christ to them. Although this understanding of love in imitation of Christ crucified was totally foreign to the cultural values of Corinth, this is the liberating attitude and lifestyle that Paul wants the Christians of Corinth to adopt for the sake of their brothers and sisters.

Reflection and discussion

- How does Paul help his readers understand their freedom and rights in new ways?

- What are some obstacles in the way of the gospel of Christ among my peers?

- What is Paul trying to teach the Corinthians who want to eat food sacrificed to idols?

Prayer

Lord God, you have blessed my life with freedom and an abundance of rights. Show me how to use my freedom and rights in ways that please you and give you glory. Give me the will to do all that I do for your sake.

LESSON 15 SESSION 4

I have become all things to all people,
that I might by all means save some.
1 CORINTHIANS 9:22

Motivation and Discipline in Ministry

1 CORINTHIANS 9:19–27 [19]*For though I am free with respect to all, I have made*
myself a slave to all, so that I might win more of them. [20]*To the Jews I became as*
a Jew, in order to win Jews. To those under the law I became as one under the law
(though I myself am not under the law) so that I might win those under the law.
[21]*To those outside the law I became as one outside the law (though I am not free*
from God's law but am under Christ's law) so that I might win those outside the
law. [22]*To the weak I became weak, so that I might win the weak. I have become all*
things to all people, that I might by all means save some. [23]*I do it all for the sake of*
the gospel, so that I may share in its blessings.

[24]*Do you not know that in a race the runners all compete, but only one receives*
the prize? Run in such a way that you may win it. [25]*Athletes exercise self-control*
in all things; they do it to receive a perishable wreath, but we an imperishable one.
[26]*So I do not run aimlessly, nor do I box as though beating the air;* [27]*but I punish*
my body and enslave it, so that after proclaiming to others I myself should not
be disqualified.

Paul explains that all other concerns are secondary in comparison to his evangelizing mission. His all-consuming goal is to "win" as many as possible to Christ (verse 19). Although he is "free," he has made himself "a slave," forgoing his freedom and rights for the sake of others. To achieve his missionary objective, Paul adapts his behavior in whatever way is necessary to transcend the ethnic and cultural barriers that impede the gospel.

Offering examples of this method of ministry, Paul says that he submits himself to the cultural structures and practices of the people he hopes to reach with the gospel (verses 20–22). When in the company of Jews, he takes on their law-observant patterns of living. Although he knows he is free and no longer bound to the works of the Jewish law, he reverts to his law-observant way of living for their sake. When among the Gentiles, he conforms his way of living to the Greek ways, yet always following the law of Christ. This new law is the pattern of Christ's self-sacrificing life lived for others. Likewise, "to the weak," he says, "I became weak." With those weak in faith or insecure in their religious practices, he makes sure to avoid any action that could be scandalous or cause them to slip back into paganism. As a support to these weak ones, he takes on their simple lifestyle, becoming a manual laborer, and refusing the patronage of the wealthy. In all these ways, Paul overcomes divisions in order to brings people of all sorts into the one community of faith.

Summarizing his method of ministry, Paul states, "I have become all things to all people, that I might by all means save some" (verse 22). His adaptability appears to some of his critics as inconsistency or even hypocrisy. However, Paul makes it clear that his versatility in ministry aims at a consistent goal: "I do it all for the sake of the gospel" (verse 23). He does whatever he can to most effectively fulfill his commission as Christ's apostle. Like Jesus himself, Paul seeks to empty himself so that he might share more fully in the condition of those he serves.

After describing his motivation and method of ministry, Paul concludes with a grand exhortation, comparing his Christian life to that of runners and boxers (verses 24–27). Although he frequently uses athletic metaphors in his letters, this one would resonate with the Corinthians because the Isthmian Games were held every other year near Corinth. As runners compete to complete the race and win the prize, Christians should live a disciplined life, focused on the things that ultimately matter. As boxers punish and enslave their own bodies in order to make every punch count, Christians should subject themselves to disciplined self-control and devote themselves to service. If the athletes in the Greek games compete to win a garland of withering leaves, how much more should Christians strive to win an imperishable crown!

Reflection and discussion

- How do I express my desire for sharing the gospel?

- How could I adapt my lifestyle and patterns of living to help others encounter Christ?

- Which athletic event from the Olympic Games is most like my own Christian life? What are the biggest challenges I encounter?

Prayer

Lord Jesus, who commissioned Paul to preach the gospel, give me his zeal for the gospel and a deep desire to win people to you. Keep my eyes on the crown of glory so that I persevere to the end.

LESSON 16 SESSION 4

God is faithful, and he will not let you be tested beyond your strength, but with the testing he will also provide the way out so that you may be able to endure it.

1 CORINTHIANS 10:13

The Exodus and the Christian Life

1 CORINTHIANS 10:1–22 *1I do not want you to be unaware, brothers and sisters, that our ancestors were all under the cloud, and all passed through the sea, 2and all were baptized into Moses in the cloud and in the sea, 3and all ate the same spiritual food, 4and all drank the same spiritual drink. For they drank from the spiritual rock that followed them, and the rock was Christ. 5Nevertheless, God was not pleased with most of them, and they were struck down in the wilderness.*

6Now these things occurred as examples for us, so that we might not desire evil as they did. 7Do not become idolaters as some of them did; as it is written, "The people sat down to eat and drink, and they rose up to play." 8We must not indulge in sexual immorality as some of them did, and twenty-three thousand fell in a single day. 9We must not put Christ to the test, as some of them did, and were destroyed by serpents. 10And do not complain as some of them did, and were destroyed by the destroyer. 11These things happened to them to serve as an example, and they were written down to instruct us, on whom the ends of the ages have come. 12So if you think you are standing, watch out that you do not fall. 13No testing has overtaken you that is not common to everyone. God is faithful, and he will not let you be tested beyond your strength, but with the testing he will also provide the way out so that you may be able to endure it.

14Therefore, my dear friends, flee from the worship of idols. 15I speak as to sensible people; judge for yourselves what I say. 16The cup of blessing that we bless, is it not a sharing in the blood of Christ? The bread that we break, is it not a sharing in the body of Christ? 17Because there is one bread, we who are many are one body, for we all partake of the one bread. 18Consider the people of Israel; are not those who eat the sacrifices partners in the altar? 19What do I imply then? That food sacrificed to idols is anything, or that an idol is anything? 20No, I imply that what pagans sacrifice, they sacrifice to demons and not to God. I do not want you to be partners with demons. 21You cannot drink the cup of the Lord and the cup of demons. You cannot partake of the table of the Lord and the table of demons. 22Or are we provoking the Lord to jealousy? Are we stronger than he?

Paul selects parallels between Israel's exodus experience and the desire of some Corinthians to eat food sacrificed to idols. Demonstrating how the Israelites violated their covenant obligations and put God to the test by consorting with idols, Paul shows the Corinthians the peril in which they place themselves by attending meals in the temples of pagan gods. The Corinthians who dare to eat food offered to idols may not fear the power of the idols, but they should certainly fear the wrath of God.

Speaking of the ancient Israelites as "our ancestors" (verse 1), Paul shows his Gentile converts that they are spiritual descendants of God's people in the Old Testament. As Christians they stand in continuity with all God has done in salvation history. Indeed, they are the covenanted and holy people of God, full heirs of all that God accomplished through their ancestors. The generation in the wilderness were delivered from Egyptian captivity and "baptized into Moses" through the cloud of the divine presence and through the parting sea (verse 2). Likewise, the Corinthians were baptized into Christ through the Holy Spirit and water. Israelites were given spiritual food and drink, manna in the desert and water from the rock, as a foreshadowing of the food and drink Christians receive in the Eucharist (verses 3–4). In fact, says Paul, "the rock was Christ," a rich metaphor of God's redeeming presence and a foreshadowing of all God's future blessings. As the source of all graces, Christ is behind both the old and the new salvation of all God's people.

By demonstrating the similarities of the Corinthians to the people of the exodus, Paul lays the foundation for his stark warning (verse 5). Despite encountering divine deliverance, sustenance, and guiding presence, and even though they experienced a prefigurement of baptism and Eucharist, they were not exempt from God's judgment when they veered from the covenant and into idolatry. The Corinthians face similar dangers and temptations in their pagan wasteland.

As Paul identifies the causes of Israel's failures, he continues to interpret the events of the exodus illumined by the light of Christ. From this perspective, these past events serve as "examples" for the Christians of Corinth (verses 6–10). Paul urges the Corinthians not to "become idolaters" as did the Israelites when they feasted and reveled in the presence of the golden calf (Exodus 32:6), not to "indulge in sexual immorality" as did the Israelites when they had relations with the women of Moab and sacrificed to their gods (Numbers 25:1–9), not to "put Christ to the test" as when the Israelites tested God and were sent a plague of serpents (Numbers 21:4–9; Psalm 78:18), and not to "complain" as when the Israelites complained and incited the wrath of God (Numbers 14:2–3). Paul wants the church in Corinth to ponder the Torah to see how these things "serve as an example" and were "written down to instruct" them (verse 11). What happened in ancient Israel now serves to teach the church, as the old age has not yet passed away and the new age is still being born. Paul assures his Corinthians of the truth that arches over the whole history of salvation: "God is faithful" (verse 13). None of the testing that the church will ever experience is beyond God's power and grace.

Paul then turns to the institution of the Eucharist by Christ in order to convince the Christians of Corinth to "flee from the worship of idols" (verse 14). The bond experienced with Christ in the Eucharist is a true communion with him: the cup we bless is a "sharing in the blood of Christ"; the bread we break is a "sharing in the body of Christ" (verse 16). This communion with Christ also establishes a real unity with other believers who share in the Eucharist. Those who partake of the "one bread" become "one body" (verse 17).

God demanded the exclusive allegiance of his people in the wilderness as he gave them spiritual food and drink, but God demands even greater fidelity from those who feed on the body and blood of Christ and become one body in him. Paul agrees that idols are not real, but the demonic powers involved in worshiping any other presence besides God are very real. Thus Paul teaches: "You cannot drink the cup of the Lord and the cup of demons. You cannot partake of the table of the Lord and the table of demons" (verse 21). The intimate union we share with Christ in Eucharist demands loyalty and the exclusive devotion of covenant.

Reflection and discussion

- Why was it so important that the new Christians in Corinth know the Old Testament?

- In what ways do the assurances Paul offers in verse 13 give confidence to the church today?

- How does Paul's discussion of the Eucharist convince Christians of the evils of eating food offered to idols?

Prayer

Faithful God, who gave your people food and drink in the wilderness, unite us in your church as we eat the body and drink the blood of your Son, Jesus Christ. Keep us faithful to you in uncompromising devotion.

LESSON 17 SESSION 4

So, whether you eat or drink, or whatever you do,
do everything for the glory of God.
1 CORINTHIANS 10:31

Accomplishing All Things for God's Glory

1 CORINTHIANS 10:23—11:1 23*"All things are lawful," but not all things are*
beneficial. "All things are lawful," but not all things build up. 24*Do not seek your*
own advantage, but that of the other. 25*Eat whatever is sold in the meat market*
without raising any question on the ground of conscience, 26*for "the earth and its*
fullness are the Lord's." 27*If an unbeliever invites you to a meal and you are dis-*
posed to go, eat whatever is set before you without raising any question on the
ground of conscience. 28*But if someone says to you, "This has been offered in sac-*
rifice," then do not eat it, out of consideration for the one who informed you, and
*for the sake of conscience—*29*I mean the other's conscience, not your own. For why*
should my liberty be subject to the judgment of someone else's conscience? 30*If I par-*
take with thankfulness, why should I be denounced because of that for which I give
thanks? 31*So, whether you eat or drink, or whatever you do, do everything for the*
glory of God. 32*Give no offense to Jews or to Greeks or to the church of God,* 33*just*
as I try to please everyone in everything I do, not seeking my own advantage, but
that of many, so that they may be saved.

11 1*Be imitators of me, as I am of Christ.*

Paul concludes his long discussion of food offered to idols with another imaginary dialogue, first quoting from the position of his dialogue partners—"All things are lawful"—and then responding with his own teaching (verse 23). If all things are lawful, then idolatrous customs can easily be excused. Paul urges the Corinthians to consider whether practices are "beneficial" and whether they "build up" the community. Because Christian life is not about being a spiritual lone ranger but a member of Christ's body, believers must always seek the advantage of others rather than their own (verse 24). The most important consideration, then, is this: "What course of action will be the most effective witness to Christ?"

Having summed up his argument, Paul now wraps up his teachings with some points about eating food outside the context of pagan temples. The Corinthians do not need to give up eating meat sold in the market or refuse invitations to dine in the homes of unbelievers (verses 25–27). Food that could possibly have associations with idols may be eaten unless it has been specifically identified as such. Avoiding all food with any associations with idols would have been impractical if not impossible in the pagan context of Corinth. The markets were flooded with such foods and it was impossible to distinguish food that came from the temples. Paul's sensible teaching does not require Christians to scrupulously investigate the history of food sold in the markets or served in the homes of others. Outside of the context of idolatry, food offered to idols becomes simply food, part of "the earth and its fullness" that belongs to the Lord. Paul does not expect the Corinthians to cut themselves off from social relationships within the city.

But Paul allows Christians to circulate in pagan society only within certain limits. They may not eat any foods that have been explicitly identified as food "offered in sacrifice" to the gods (verse 28). In this case, concern for others must overrule the right to eat as one pleases. They must abstain from such food because of their care for the consciences of others. Paul helps the Corinthians keep their evangelizing mission in mind when considering this issue. Eating food offered to idols compromises the Christians' confession of the one God, fails to lead unbelievers away from honoring pagan gods, and invites the influence of demonic powers by honoring false gods. Believers should always seek opportunities to witness their Christian faith.

Paul adds two rhetorical questions that could be posed as objections to his teachings (verses 29–30). He places these questions in the mouths of his dialogue partners: Why should my freedom be limited by the conscience of another? Why should I be criticized for eating food that I consume with thanksgiving? Paul's discussion thus far and his final imperatives provide clear responses to these objections. All questions of eating and drinking or anything else may be discerned by the ultimate principle: "Whatever you do, do everything for the glory of God" (verse 31). This Christian principle provides a remarkable contrast to the opening slogan, "All things are lawful."

Paul urges his community never to cause other Christians to falter in faith or to hamper others from accepting the gospel (verse 32). Giving "no offense to Jews" means doing nothing that might give them the impression that Christian teaching condones idolatry or undermines the confession of one God. Giving no offense "to Greeks" means doing nothing that could confirm their resistance to the gospel. And giving no offense "to the church of God" means doing nothing that could give Christians reason to weaken in faith or fall back into idolatry. Bringing glory to God means always behaving in ways that lead others to a saving relationship with Jesus Christ.

As an apostle, Paul understands himself to be the norm of behavior for his churches (verses 31; 11:1). As Christ did not seek his own advantage, but that of others, so Paul desires to always look for openings to help others come to saving faith. So as Christians follow the example of Paul and the greater example of Christ, they relinquish their personal rights and freedoms so as to always proclaim the gospel by embodying it in their own lives.

Reflection and discussion

- In what ways might I be putting obstacles in the way of others coming to know Jesus Christ?

- What advice of Paul helps me discern whether or not an action is beneficial to others and builds up the church?

- In what ways might I surrender my personal rights and freedoms in order to give witness to Christ?

- What practical results in my own life could come from following Paul's rule, "Do everything for the glory of God"?

Prayer

Lord Jesus Christ, you call all your disciples to proclaim the gospel with their lives. Show me how to help take away the obstacles from the lives of others and lead them to a saving relationship with you.

LESSON 18 SESSION 4

Nevertheless, in the Lord woman is not independent of man or man independent of woman. For just as woman came from man, so man comes through woman; but all things come from God.

1 CORINTHIANS 11:11–12

Male and Female in Public Worship

1 CORINTHIANS 11:2–16 2*I commend you because you remember me in every-*
thing and maintain the traditions just as I handed them on to you. 3*But I want you*
to understand that Christ is the head of every man, and the husband is the head
of his wife, and God is the head of Christ. 4*Any man who prays or prophesies with*
something on his head disgraces his head, 5*but any woman who prays or proph-*
esies with her head unveiled disgraces her head—it is one and the same thing as
having her head shaved. 6*For if a woman will not veil herself, then she should cut*
off her hair; but if it is disgraceful for a woman to have her hair cut off or to be
shaved, she should wear a veil. 7*For a man ought not to have his head veiled, since*
he is the image and reflection of God; but woman is the reflection of man. 8*Indeed,*
man was not made from woman, but woman from man. 9*Neither was man cre-*
ated for the sake of woman, but woman for the sake of man. 10*For this reason a*
woman ought to have a symbol of authority on her head, because of the angels.
11*Nevertheless, in the Lord woman is not independent of man or man independent*
of woman. 12*For just as woman came from man, so man comes through woman;*
but all things come from God. 13*Judge for yourselves: is it proper for a woman to*
pray to God with her head unveiled? 14*Does not nature itself teach you that if a*
man wears long hair, it is degrading to him, 15*but if a woman has long hair, it is her*

glory? For her hair is given to her for a covering. [16]*But if anyone is disposed to be contentious—we have no such custom, nor do the churches of God.*

Although Paul taught his communities that unity in Christ transcends the divisions between male and female (Galatians 3:28), some in Corinth were misapplying that teaching, seeking to eradicate the traditional distinctions between men and women in Christian worship. So, after commending the community for maintaining the traditions that Paul had handed on to them, Paul begins to explain that the differences between men and women are part of God's purposes in creation and should not be obscured when the church gathers. In the Lord there is both a mutuality and a distinctiveness between the two sexes.

Paul focuses on the issue of head coverings when a man or a woman "prays or prophesies" in the communal assembly (verses 4–5). He takes for granted that both men and women were performing the same public role in their religious services. Yet, Paul insists that men should not cover their heads and women should cover their heads. His extensive explanation for this seemingly minor distinction indicates the importance of maintaining traditional norms. Greek women ordinarily wore a headscarf in social life, except when in their own home or the homes of their relatives. Women who went uncovered in public gave nonverbal clues that they were "available," whereas covering the head was a sign of modesty. So, by remaining uncovered during public worship, the women of Corinth were either expressing their liberating equality in Christ or they considered the house churches to be domestic rather than public settings. Paul's purpose, then, is not to develop a theology of gender, but simply to correct an inappropriate practice that could tarnish the church's reputation.

Using the word "head" in a metaphorical sense, Paul establishes the following order: God, Christ, man/husband, woman/wife (verse 3). The order is not intended to denote a hierarchical rank, or to suggest authority and subordination, since Paul would never say that Christ is secondary or subordinate to God. The order, rather, indicates that one is prior to the other: as the origin of all reality, God is prior to Christ; as the one through whom all things were made, Christ is prior to man; and man is prior to woman according to

Genesis, since woman is made from man (verse 8). Thus, the metaphorical sense of "the head" can be understood as "ahead." God is ahead of Christ; Christ is ahead of man; man is ahead of woman.

Paul then argues that the man who worships with a head covering, a practice associated with offering pagan sacrifices, dishonors Christ (verse 4). Likewise, the woman who worships without a head covering, thus letting her hair down in a public gathering, brings shame to her husband (verse 5). To reinforce his case, Paul submits that man is the image of God, but woman is the reflected glory of man (verse 7). She completes the man as well as completes creation. Thus, Paul asserts, "a woman ought to have a symbol of authority on her head" (verse 10). The head covering signifies her right as a Christian woman to have a public role in the assembly, a right she did not formerly possess apart from Christ. She might appear to be usurping a male role by praying and prophesying and consequently needs a symbol of her new authority. The woman's new status in Christ must be clarified "because of the angels," who are always present when the church worships and serve as guardians of the order and beauty of divine worship.

Paul confirms that his teachings do not imply an inferior place for women. As Christians, women and men are interdependent: "In the Lord woman is not independent of man or man independent of woman" (verse 11). Although men and women are equal, they must still honor their God-given place in creation. Paul's statement that woman comes from man, suggesting the male's priority in creation, is now counterbalanced by the fact that now man comes "through" woman (verse 12). Because all men are born from women, males now depend on females for their existence.

Concluding his case, Paul raises again the issue of women's head coverings in public worship and urges his readers to judge for themselves (verse 13). But he adds one further argument. Nature has given women their hair as a cover, while men's short and receding hair indicates it is not a cover for them (verses 14–15). Because of the Greek cultural norms, the long hair of a man is his shame, while the long hair of a woman is her glory. The shaven head of a woman is an abnormal condition that removes nature's covering and is a sign of shame in the Greek culture. Women, therefore, ought to follow nature's lead and cover their heads.

Finally, Paul urges the Corinthians to simply follow the universal practice of the other churches throughout his mission (verse 16). That alone should cause them to reconsider the practice of women who unveil their heads and let down their hair in public worship. Clearly Paul's instructions are tied to the cultural norms of the Greek world of the first century, and Christians today are not obliged to follow the directions literally. However, Paul's concern that Christians honor sexual decorum and dress modestly in worship is broadly applicable in every age.

Reflection and discussion

- Paul seems to suggest that men and women are both equal and distinct and that their roles are both complementary and reciprocal. What evidence leads to this understanding?

- Why is Paul so insistent on the issue of head coverings for the Corinthians?

- What might be the intention of women today who prefer to cover their head with a veil during liturgical worship?

- Paul spotlights the dependence of men and women on each other by saying, "Just as woman came from man, so man comes through woman" (verse 12). What are other ways in which men and women are dependent on each other?

- In what way should this passage be practically applied to the church today?

Prayer

Creator God, who made man and woman in your own image, show us how to treat one another with dignity. May man and woman work and pray together in the church for your glory.

SUGGESTIONS FOR FACILITATORS, GROUP SESSION 4

1. Welcome group members and ask if anyone has any questions, announcements, or requests.

2. You may want to pray this prayer as a group:
   Faithful God, who provided deliverance, sustenance, and guidance for your people in the wilderness, you promised not to test us beyond our strength as we face dangers and temptations. Show us how to use our freedom in ways that give you glory and that respond to the needs of others. As you called your servant Paul to proclaim the gospel, instill in us a desire to bring others to a saving relationship with you and to persevere in the calling you have given to each of us.

3. Ask one or more of the following questions:
   - What is the most difficult part of this study for you?
   - What insights stand out to you from the lessons this week?

4. Discuss lessons 13 through 18. Choose one or more of the questions for reflection and discussion from each lesson to discuss as a group. You may want to ask group members which question was most challenging or helpful to them as you review each lesson.

5. Keep the discussion moving, but allow time for the questions that provoke the most discussion. Encourage the group members to use "I" language in their responses.

6. After talking over each lesson, instruct group members to complete lessons 19 through 24 on their own during the six days before the next group meeting. They should write out their own answers to the questions as preparation for next week's session.

7. Ask the group what encouragement they need for the coming week. Ask the members to pray for the needs of one another during the week.

8. Conclude by praying aloud together the prayer at the end of one of the lessons discussed. You may choose to conclude the prayer by asking members to pray aloud any requests they may have.

LESSON 19 SESSION 5

Whoever, therefore, eats the bread or drinks the cup of the Lord in an unworthy manner will be answerable for the body and blood of the Lord. 1 CORINTHIANS 11:27

Discerning the Body at the Lord's Supper

1 CORINTHIANS 11:17–34 [17]*Now in the following instructions I do not commend you, because when you come together it is not for the better but for the worse.*
[18]For, to begin with, when you come together as a church, I hear that there are divisions among you; and to some extent I believe it. [19]Indeed, there have to be factions
among you, for only so will it become clear who among you are genuine. [20]When
you come together, it is not really to eat the Lord's supper. [21]For when the time
comes to eat, each of you goes ahead with your own supper, and one goes hungry and another becomes drunk. [22]What! Do you not have homes to eat and drink in? Or do you show contempt for the church of God and humiliate those who have nothing? What should I say to you? Should I commend you? In this matter I do not commend you!

[23]For I received from the Lord what I also handed on to you, that the Lord Jesus on the night when he was betrayed took a loaf of bread, [24]and when he had given
thanks, he broke it and said, "This is my body that is for you. Do this in remembrance of me." [25]In the same way he took the cup also, after supper, saying, "This
cup is the new covenant in my blood. Do this, as often as you drink it, in remembrance of me." [26]For as often as you eat this bread and drink the cup, you proclaim
the Lord's death until he comes.

27 Whoever, therefore, eats the bread or drinks the cup of the Lord in an unworthy manner will be answerable for the body and blood of the Lord. 28 Examine yourselves, and only then eat of the bread and drink of the cup. 29 For all who eat and drink without discerning the body, eat and drink judgment against themselves. 30 For this reason many of you are weak and ill, and some have died. 31 But if we judged ourselves, we would not be judged. 32 But when we are judged by the Lord, we are disciplined so that we may not be condemned along with the world.

33 So then, my brothers and sisters, when you come together to eat, wait for one another. 34 If you are hungry, eat at home, so that when you come together, it will not be for your condemnation. About the other things I will give instructions when I come.

The Lord's Supper, the name Paul uses for the Christian Eucharist, was celebrated in Corinth in the context of a meal, as was the Jewish Passover and the Last Supper of Jesus. The assemblies consisted of rich and poor, slaves and free persons, women and men, all coming together "as a church" in the larger homes of the city (verse 18). But this central and defining celebration on the Lord's Day became plagued with problems. Divisions and factions developed. Some went hungry while others indulged (verse 21). The poor were humiliated because they had nothing to eat (verse 22). Paul was horrified that social hierarchies and economic factions had infiltrated the church's central act of worship. The assembly was not even worthy to be called "the Lord's Supper" (verse 20). The words and gestures given by Christ to his church had become empty because the community was no longer doing what Jesus did, giving his life in self-emptying love. The Eucharist was to be a meal of generous self-giving, the expression of a community in which people formerly divided by race, class, and gender became one body in Christ.

Paul reminds the church of the words and actions of Jesus at the Last Supper in order to correct their understanding and practice of the Eucharist. Jesus pronounced that the broken bread is "my body that is for you" and that the cup is "the new covenant in my blood" (verses 24–25). Christ's redemptive death for others and his inauguration of the new covenant is the central meaning of their worship together. The Corinthians must learn to celebrate the Lord's Supper in a way that demonstrates how profoundly the Lord's death has changed the condition of people's relationships with one another and the responsibilities of people bound with God in covenant obligations.

Paul then adds his own understanding of the meaning of Eucharist: "For as often as you eat this bread and drink the cup, you proclaim the Lord's death until he comes" (verse 26). The Eucharist proclaims the past, the redemptive death of Jesus; the present, the community that experiences salvation in eating and drinking his body and blood; and the future, the glorious coming of Christ. Looking backward to the Lord's death and forward to his return, all of salvation history comes together in the timeless, sacramental moment.

With this understanding, eating and drinking the Lord's body and blood has implications that no other eating and drinking ever does. Sharing the Eucharist "in an unworthy manner" means eating and drinking in a way that causes division, shows disregard for the poor and hungry, and forgets the obligations of the covenant (verse 27). Self-centeredness, individualism, and arrogance makes one "answerable for the body and blood of the Lord," that is, responsible for his death and guilty of dishonoring his presence in the Eucharist.

So, Christians who are preparing to share communion in Christ must "examine" themselves to make sure they are in a fit state to partake of the holy supper (verse 28). It is fraught with spiritual peril if they treat this sacred meal in a careless manner. Those who eat and drink at the church's worship "without discerning the body" eat and drink their own judgment (verse 29). Worthy communion means realizing the presence of the living Christ and the corporate unity of all who share his life.

Reflection and discussion

- Paul claims that when the Corinthian church gathers, it is not the Lord's Supper that they come to eat, but their own supper of indulgence and indifference. How does he want the church to change?

- In what ways does the Eucharist bring together the past, present, and future?

- How should I "examine" myself in order to "eat of the bread and drink of the cup" worthily (verse 28)?

- If the Lord's Supper is intended to memorialize Christ's sacrifice, what should be the character and climate of our Sunday Eucharist?

Prayer

Living Lord, who handed on the Eucharist to your church through the apostles, may we proclaim your saving death until you return in glory. Help me to prepare to worship you by reflecting your self-giving love for all people.

LESSON 20 **SESSION 5**

All these are activated by one and the same Spirit, who allots to each one individually just as the Spirit chooses. 1 CORINTHIANS 12:11

Unity and Diversity of Spiritual Gifts

1 CORINTHIANS 12:1–11 [1]*Now concerning spiritual gifts, brothers and sisters, I do not want you to be uninformed.* [2]*You know that when you were pagans, you were enticed and led astray to idols that could not speak.* [3]*Therefore I want you to understand that no one speaking by the Spirit of God ever says "Let Jesus be cursed!" and no one can say "Jesus is Lord" except by the Holy Spirit.*

[4]*Now there are varieties of gifts, but the same Spirit;* [5]*and there are varieties of services, but the same Lord;* [6]*and there are varieties of activities, but it is the same God who activates all of them in everyone.* [7]*To each is given the manifestation of the Spirit for the common good.* [8]*To one is given through the Spirit the utterance of wisdom, and to another the utterance of knowledge according to the same Spirit,* [9]*to another faith by the same Spirit, to another gifts of healing by the one Spirit,* [10]*to another the working of miracles, to another prophecy, to another the discernment of spirits, to another various kinds of tongues, to another the interpretation of tongues.* [11]*All these are activated by one and the same Spirit, who allots to each one individually just as the Spirit chooses.*

The next pastoral issue to which Paul responds is that of "spiritual gifts," the manifestations of God's grace within the church. It seems that a self-serving competitiveness threatened to contaminate the expression of spiritual gifts within the community. Whereas the Corinthians limited these expressions of the Spirit to a few impressive gifts, Paul helps them understand that all Christians are instilled with the Holy Spirit and that everyone contributes their own gifts for building up the whole community. No one should feel superior for possessing a particular spiritual attribute, and no one should feel left out for lacking a particular gift. The Spirit determines who gets what gift and apportions them, not according to the value of the recipient, but according to the needs of the community.

Paul begins by reminding the Corinthians of their pagan past, when they had been led in procession to lifeless idols who were unable to respond to their desires (verse 2). Now they are imbued with the life-giving Spirit as they profess "Jesus is Lord" (verse 3). All who make this baptismal confession—turning from their past blindness, declaring their absolute allegiance to Jesus, and accepting his authority over every aspect of their lives—are led by the Holy Spirit and receive a range of spiritual gifts.

In three parallel statements, Paul declares that there are varieties of gifts, but the same Spirit; varieties of services, but the same Lord; and varieties of activities, but the same God who activates all of them in everyone (verses 4–6). The rich diversity of the divine presence among believers—experienced as Spirit, Lord, and God—is the foundation for the abundant variety of gifts in the church. Great variety exists within the unity of the church because the source of the church's life is the one God manifested in three divine persons.

These three categories—gifts, services, and activities—are not hard and fast. Each of these phenomena can also be identified as "the manifestation of the Spirit" (verse 7). The emphasis is on the variety of ways the Spirit is manifested. The source of the gifts is not the individual talents of each person or the person's spiritual accomplishments. These many gifts are given to individuals so that they may benefit others and serve the whole body.

Paul offers nine examples of these gifts of the Spirit, expressing them as common occurrences in the church (verses 8–10). The list is not exhaustive and simply represents the diversity of the Spirit's manifestations. These are typical gifts relevant to the church in Corinth. Lists of different gifts are found in Paul's letters to other communities. Notice that wisdom and knowledge are not gifts until they have become "utterances" of wisdom and knowledge to benefit the church. Gifts do not need to be spectacular to be manifestations of the

Spirit. The same community that prized the intellectual gift of uttering wisdom also valued the highly emotional gift of speaking in tongues. Healings, miracles, and prophetic speech seem to be regular events within the community.

The church Paul envisions possesses a wide spectrum of gifts within the community. This rich diversity of spiritual gifts within the individual members of the church is directed by the same divine source, the Holy Spirit (verse 11). The power of God's Spirit is palpably present, working to create unity through the many complementary gifts provided by every member of the community.

Reflection and discussion

- How would I go about discerning whether a particular ability was truly a gift of the Holy Spirit?

- How is the unity and diversity of the church's gifts related to the Father, Son, and Holy Spirit?

- What gift, service, or activity do I have to offer to the church?

Prayer

Come, Holy Spirit, living within the community of the baptized, fill your church with gifts in abundance. Teach me to proclaim with my life that Jesus is Lord, and help me discern the gifts you have given me to serve others.

LESSON 21 SESSION 5

**If one member suffers, all suffer together with it;
if one member is honored, all rejoice together with it.**
1 CORINTHIANS 12:26

Members of the Body of Christ

1 CORINTHIANS 12:12–31 [12]*For just as the body is one and has many members, and all the members of the body, though many, are one body, so it is with Christ.* [13]*For in the one Spirit we were all baptized into one body—Jews or Greeks, slaves or free—and we were all made to drink of one Spirit.*

[14]*Indeed, the body does not consist of one member but of many.* [15]*If the foot would say, "Because I am not a hand, I do not belong to the body," that would not make it any less a part of the body.* [16]*And if the ear would say, "Because I am not an eye, I do not belong to the body," that would not make it any less a part of the body.* [17]*If the whole body were an eye, where would the hearing be? If the whole body were hearing, where would the sense of smell be?* [18]*But as it is, God arranged the members in the body, each one of them, as he chose.* [19]*If all were a single member, where would the body be?* [20]*As it is, there are many members, yet one body.* [21]*The eye cannot say to the hand, "I have no need of you," nor again the head to the feet, "I have no need of you."* [22]*On the contrary, the members of the body that seem to be weaker are indispensable,* [23]*and those members of the body that we think less honorable we clothe with greater honor, and our less respectable members are treated with greater respect;* [24]*whereas our more respectable members do not need this. But God has so arranged the body, giving the greater honor to the inferior member,* [25]*that there may be no dissension within the body, but the*

members may have the same care for one another. 26*If one member suffers, all suffer*
together with it; if one member is honored, all rejoice together with it.
27*Now you are the body of Christ and individually members of it.* 28*And God*
has appointed in the church first apostles, second prophets, third teachers; then
deeds of power, then gifts of healing, forms of assistance, forms of leadership, vari-
ous kinds of tongues. 29*Are all apostles? Are all prophets? Are all teachers? Do all*
work miracles? 30*Do all possess gifts of healing? Do all speak in tongues? Do all*
interpret? 31*But strive for the greater gifts. And I will show you a still more excel-*
lent way.

Continuing to respond to the issue of spiritual gifts within the church and addressing the scourge of factionalism, Paul presents his well-known metaphor of the church as "the body of Christ." He begins by comparing the human body, which is essentially a unity though it is made up of many diverse parts and functions, to the community. But he quickly applies the body image to Christ himself: "so it is with Christ" (verse 12). Through this elaborate image, he describes the multiplicity, interdependence, and importance of all the members of the church.

The great variety of believers is bound in a living unity with the risen Christ. In him, the great diversity of the community and its many gifts becomes purposeful and beneficial. This unity in the body of Christ is realized through the work of the Holy Spirit: "In the one Spirit we were all baptized into one body" (verse 13). Baptism into Christ washes away the ethnic and social barriers that previously separated people. Through the power of the Spirit, even extreme incompatibility—Jews or Greeks, slaves or free people—is superseded and overcome. What may polarize the world must not divide the church.

Paul's elaboration of the body metaphor emphasizes the necessity of diversity in the church. The essence of the body is its differentiation into diverse and complementary parts. Without this separation, the body could not function. By imagining scenarios in which various body parts ridiculously secede from the body, Paul shows how each member is essential to the whole (verses 15–17). Because each part of the body has its own unique purpose in the functioning of the whole, no member of the church should ever think that his or her contribution is unimportant. In fact, this design is set within the divine plan: "God arranged the members in the body, each one of them, as he chose" (verse 18).

How foolish it would be if the eye said to the hand, or if the head said to the feet, "I have no need of you" (verse 21). "Eye" and "head" are obvious metaphors for those in leadership roles who are likely better educated and more affluent. The "hands" and "feet" represent the laboring class or slaves. But all the members of the body need one another; no one should look down upon another. On the contrary, "the members of the body that seem to be weaker are indispensable" (verse 22), and those who seem to be strong ignore the weak at their own peril. If there is dissension and division among the members, the whole body suffers. Paul imagines a unifying synergy within the church in which all members share the joys and sorrows of one another (verse 26).

Paul applies his image of the body to the variety of the Spirit's gifts within the body of Christ. He lists eight examples of various ministries and functions within the community (verse 28). Some of them are the same as his previous list of gifts (12:8–10); others are different. His rhetorical questions emphasize that everyone cannot have the same gift, and no one can have all the gifts (verses 29–30). Through his elaborate metaphor of the body of Christ, Paul corrects a distorted understanding of spiritual gifts and the overemphasis on certain conspicuous gifts that some felt set them apart and above the other members of the church. Members of the body should humbly accept their gifts without pretentiously flaunting them, belittling another's, or envying another's. Paul urges the church to strive for solidarity, not uniformity. This is only possible when the diversity of the Spirit's gifts is honored, and the Spirit is allowed to activate the various manifestations of God's grace within the living body of Christ.

Reflection and discussion

- In what ways does Paul's image of the body of Christ turn the values and priorities of the world upside down?

- Paul says, "If one member suffers, all suffer together with it; if one member is honored, all rejoice together with it." How do I experience this in my own physical body? How does this apply to the church?

- In what ways am I most aware of the power of the Holy Spirit working within me?

Prayer

Come, Holy Spirit, who distributes manifold gifts within the church, help me envision my life as a member of the body of Christ. Give me a deep desire to break down division and to serve others in love.

LESSON 22 SESSION 5

For now we see in a mirror, dimly, but then we will see face to face. Now I know only in part; then I will know fully, even as I have been fully known. 1 CORINTHIANS 13:12

The Character of Genuine Love

1 CORINTHIANS 13:1–13 *1 If I speak in the tongues of mortals and of angels, but*
do not have love, I am a noisy gong or a clanging cymbal. 2 And if I have prophetic
powers, and understand all mysteries and all knowledge, and if I have all faith, so
as to remove mountains, but do not have love, I am nothing. 3 If I give away all my
possessions, and if I hand over my body so that I may boast, but do not have love,
I gain nothing.

4 Love is patient; love is kind; love is not envious or boastful or arrogant 5 or
rude. It does not insist on its own way; it is not irritable or resentful; 6 it does not
rejoice in wrongdoing, but rejoices in the truth. 7 It bears all things, believes all
things, hopes all things, endures all things.

8 Love never ends. But as for prophecies, they will come to an end; as for tongues,
they will cease; as for knowledge, it will come to an end. 9 For we know only in part,
and we prophesy only in part; 10 but when the complete comes, the partial will
come to an end. 11 When I was a child, I spoke like a child, I thought like a child, I
reasoned like a child; when I became an adult, I put an end to childish ways. 12 For
now we see in a mirror, dimly, but then we will see face to face. Now I know only in
part; then I will know fully, even as I have been fully known. 13 And now faith, hope,
and love abide, these three; and the greatest of these is love.

Paul's timeless tribute to love forms an integral part of his corrective instructions on spiritual gifts in chapters 12—14. He introduces this teaching on genuine love as he concludes his discourse on the body of Christ: "I will show you a still more excellent way" (12:31). Here he shows that love is the "excellent way" in which all gifts should be actualized. The heart of his teaching (verses 4–7) is surrounded by two sections that relate the gifts of the Spirit to love (verses 1–3, 8–13). As valuable as the gifts are, they are worthless if not exercised in love. As Christ is to the many members of his body, the church, so love is to the diversity of the spiritual gifts.

Recalling the gifts highlighted in the last chapter—tongues, prophecy, and knowledge—Paul demonstrates how meaningless these gifts are without love (verses 1–3). Only when exercised with love do they become useful in building up the church. Speaking in tongues becomes a clamorous noise if not done in love. Prophetic utterances, understanding revealed mysteries, and extraordinary faith mean nothing without love. Even extreme self-sacrifice for others, when done without love, achieves nothing.

The love (*agape*, in Greek) of which Paul speaks is not like other types of love that might be described as an inner feeling of the heart or a personal emotion. This love is other-directed and can be defined only by what it does and does not do (verses 4–7). Love is active and dynamic. It is the nature of love to show itself in tangible ways, to prove itself in action, to demonstrate itself for others. Paul's description of love corresponds to the Christian experience of God's love, the love that God demonstrated through the cross of Christ.

Paul's description of love is tailor-made for the Corinthians in order to highlight their lack of love. Omitting the negative in each clause offers an accurate description of the behavior Paul has been criticizing throughout the letter. The Corinthians are indeed envious, boastful, and arrogant, puffed up with their own self-importance. They are rude, irritable, and resentful in their treatment of the weak and poor. But these negative characteristics also fit the sinful behavior of humanity, and the universal character of love provides all people an ideal to which they can aspire.

There will come a time when even the gifts of the Spirit will come to an end, along with everything else we have acquired in this life (verse 8). Prophecies, tongues, and knowledge have a built-in obsolescence and will give way to what is beyond themselves. All the gifts are suitable only for this time in which humanity lives at the threshold, leaving behind the old era and standing at the entry of the promised age that is already upon us. Paul presents three contrasts—partial/complete (verse 10), childhood/adulthood (verse 11), and now/then (verse 12)—that correspond to increasing maturity in Christ. In our present state of immaturity, we understand and experience the things of God only in ways that are incomplete. We see now only an obscure reflection of reality—like looking into an ancient mirror—but then we will know God fully in a face-to-face encounter.

Although prophecies, tongues, and knowledge are transient, "faith, hope, and love abide" (verse 13). The gifts of the Spirit come and go in the church, and they are not essential to the Christian life. But faith, hope, and love are indispensable for the Christian life and must remain through the passing of time. Of these three, love is eternal. As the essential reflection of God's nature, "love never ends," and what we do in love remains forever.

Reflection and discussion

- In what ways does Paul's understanding of love differ from the way it is often understood in our culture today?

- Why does Paul place this teaching on genuine love immediately after his teaching on the body of Christ and the diversity of spiritual gifts (chapter 12)?

- Why do the actions of Christians become genuine only when they are done for love, with love, and in love?

- Which characteristic of love could make my Christian actions more mature and complete?

- What hope does Paul offer to the community through this teaching?

Prayer

Eternal Father, who has demonstrated true love through the cross of your Son, show me how to love as you love. Guide me as I seek to mature and perfect the love I give to others.

LESSON 23 SESSION 5

**I will pray with the spirit, but I will pray
with the mind also; I will sing praise with the spirit,
but I will sing praise with the mind also.**
1 CORINTHIANS 14:15

Priorities and Clarity in Worship

1 CORINTHIANS 14:1–25 [1]*Pursue love and strive for the spiritual gifts, and*
especially that you may prophesy. [2]*For those who speak in a tongue do not speak*
to other people but to God; for nobody understands them, since they are speaking
mysteries in the Spirit. [3]*On the other hand, those who prophesy speak to other*
people for their upbuilding and encouragement and consolation. [4]*Those who speak*
in a tongue build up themselves, but those who prophesy build up the church. [5]*Now*
I would like all of you to speak in tongues, but even more to prophesy. One who
prophesies is greater than one who speaks in tongues, unless someone interprets, so
that the church may be built up.

[6]*Now, brothers and sisters, if I come to you speaking in tongues, how will I*
benefit you unless I speak to you in some revelation or knowledge or prophecy or
teaching? [7]*It is the same way with lifeless instruments that produce sound, such as*
the flute or the harp. If they do not give distinct notes, how will anyone know what
is being played? [8]*And if the bugle gives an indistinct sound, who will get ready for*
battle? [9]*So with yourselves; if in a tongue you utter speech that is not intelligible,*
how will anyone know what is being said? For you will be speaking into the air.
[10]*There are doubtless many different kinds of sounds in the world, and nothing is*
without sound. [11]*If then I do not know the meaning of a sound, I will be a foreigner*

to the speaker and the speaker a foreigner to me. 12*So with yourselves; since you are*
eager for spiritual gifts, strive to excel in them for building up the church.

13*Therefore, one who speaks in a tongue should pray for the power to inter-*
pret. 14*For if I pray in a tongue, my spirit prays but my mind is unproductive.*
15*What should I do then? I will pray with the spirit, but I will pray with the mind*
also; I will sing praise with the spirit, but I will sing praise with the mind also.
16*Otherwise, if you say a blessing with the spirit, how can anyone in the position*
of an outsider say the "Amen" to your thanksgiving, since the outsider does not
know what you are saying? 17*For you may give thanks well enough, but the other*
person is not built up. 18*I thank God that I speak in tongues more than all of you;*
19*nevertheless, in church I would rather speak five words with my mind, in order to*
instruct others also, than ten thousand words in a tongue.

20*Brothers and sisters, do not be children in your thinking; rather, be infants in*
evil, but in thinking be adults. 21*In the law it is written,*

"By people of strange tongues
and by the lips of foreigners
I will speak to this people;
yet even then they will not listen to me,"

says the Lord. 22*Tongues, then, are a sign not for believers but for unbelievers, while*
prophecy is not for unbelievers but for believers. 23*If, therefore, the whole church*
comes together and all speak in tongues, and outsiders or unbelievers enter, will
they not say that you are out of your mind? 24*But if all prophesy, an unbeliever*
or outsider who enters is reproved by all and called to account by all. 25*After the*
secrets of the unbeliever's heart are disclosed, that person will bow down before
God and worship him, declaring, "God is really among you."

After teaching about the nature of spiritual gifts and the "excellent way" of love, Paul applies his instruction to the assembly gathered for worship in Corinth. Comparing the spiritual gifts of tongues and prophecy, Paul states their primary difference: "Those who speak in a tongue do not speak to other people but to God" (verse 2); and "those who prophesy speak to other people for their upbuilding and encouragement and consolation" (verse 3). Tongues is a language of prayerful praise addressed to God, a form of Spirit-guided communication beyond the realm of rational speech. Prophecy is Spirit-guided speech through which God's plan for the community and God's will for individuals is made known. Although it may address future events, it is primarily focused on present reality in ways that bring encouragement, consolation, conviction, or repentance.

Those who speak in tongues build up their own faith, whereas "those who prophesy build up the church" (verse 4). Tongues are oriented toward communion with God, prophecy toward communication for the sake of others in order to edify the assembly. Although Paul recommends speaking in tongues, he encourages prophecy as the greater gift (verse 5). Intelligible speech is necessary for the common good of the assembly, whereas unintelligible tongues must either be interpreted into comprehensible language or reserved for private prayer.

Speaking in tongues is not helpful for the work of evangelization; only the intelligible speech of revelation, knowledge, prophecy, or teaching will lead others to faith (verse 6). Paul uses three analogies to make his case for excluding uninterpreted tongues from the communal worship. First, musical instruments will all make noise when piped or plucked, but they will play a discernible melody only when the mind of the player gives them distinct pitches (verse 7). Second, a bugle cannot call troops to battle with only a garbled sound. It serves its purpose and calls people to action only when sounded distinctly (verse 8). Third, the different languages of the world erect barriers of alienation between people, making them foreigners to one another (verse 11). With these examples, Paul urges the Corinthians to excel in the spiritual gifts that build up the church and help it achieve its evangelizing purpose (verse 12).

Paul's purpose is not to persuade the Corinthians to choose the gift of prophecy over that of tongues but to integrate the "spirit" and the "mind" (verses 14–15). Through Paul's spirit, he communicates with God; through his mind, he communicates with human beings. The mind organizes the thoughts and feelings associated with prayerful communication with God into comprehensible language. Both the spirit and the mind must be active in prayer and song, in tongues and prophecies, in order to worship God and build up the community.

Paul is not teaching that praising God in tongues is completely inappropriate in the assembly. But prayer in the spirit must be interpreted with the mind. Worshippers should offer thanksgiving to God in the spirit, but in such a way that the congregation knows what they are thanking God for and when to suitably respond with their "Amen" (verses 16–17). Paul himself admits, "I speak in tongues more than all of you," but he refrains from employing this gift "in church" because he would rather speak "five words" with his mind in order to give instruction to the congregation than "ten thousand words in a tongue" (verses 18–19).

A fascination with spiritual gifts as an end in themselves is childish, while a mature perspective considers the impact of these gifts on others, particularly on those who do not yet believe in the gospel (verses 20–25). If unbelievers enter the assembly and find believers speaking in tongues, the outsiders will assume that the Christians are just a frenzied sect caught up in spiritual ecstasy, one more option in the religious marketplace of Corinth. But if the outsiders come and find the members of the church prophesying in clear, intelligible language, they will encounter God's word and perhaps be convinced of their true condition before God. If these unbelievers are truly cut to the heart, they will "bow down before God and worship him." Thus, genuine prophetic speech is a powerful instrument for evangelization.

Reflection and discussion

- Still today, many falsely associate the work of the Holy Spirit more with emotional phenomenon than rational reflection on the word of God. How do I experience God's Spirit in my study of this letter?

- Why is it important to pray and worship God with both "my spirit" and "my mind"?

- How does Paul use a comparison to musical instruments to stress the importance of spiritual gifts for building up the church?

- What difference would it make in the way I participate in my church's liturgy if I considered its impact on outsiders and unbelievers who might enter the church?

Prayer

Risen Lord, who is powerfully present in the assembly as we worship the Father, give me the gift of speaking in ways that make use of my spirit and my mind, so that my words may bring encouragement, challenge, and comfort to others.

LESSON 24 SESSION 5

So, my friends, be eager to prophesy, and do not forbid speaking in tongues; but all things should be done decently and in order.

1 CORINTHIANS 14:39

Instructions for Orderly Worship

1 CORINTHIANS 14:26–40 [26]*What should be done then, my friends? When you come together, each one has a hymn, a lesson, a revelation, a tongue, or an interpretation. Let all things be done for building up.* [27]*If anyone speaks in a tongue, let there be only two or at most three, and each in turn; and let one interpret.* [28]*But if there is no one to interpret, let them be silent in church and speak to themselves and to God.* [29]*Let two or three prophets speak, and let the others weigh what is said.* [30]*If a revelation is made to someone else sitting nearby, let the first person be silent.* [31]*For you can all prophesy one by one, so that all may learn and all be encouraged.* [32]*And the spirits of prophets are subject to the prophets,* [33]*for God is a God not of disorder but of peace. (As in all the churches of the saints,* [34]*women should be silent in the churches. For they are not permitted to speak, but should be subordinate, as the law also says.* [35]*If there is anything they desire to know, let them ask their husbands at home. For it is shameful for a woman to speak in church.* [36]*Or did the word of God originate with you? Or are you the only ones it has reached?)*

[37]*Anyone who claims to be a prophet, or to have spiritual powers, must acknowledge that what I am writing to you is a command of the Lord.* [38]*Anyone who does not recognize this is not to be recognized.* [39]*So, my friends, be eager to prophesy, and do not forbid speaking in tongues;* [40]*but all things should be done decently and in order.*

Having explained the importance of using spiritual gifts for the edification of the assembly, Paul now offers some guidelines for how prayer meetings should be conducted. He advises the Corinthians to give voice to an abundance of spiritual gifts distributed over a wide variety of persons: hymns, biblical teachings, words of prophecy, praise of God in tongues, and interpretations (verse 26). Because such an expression of spiritual gifts can threaten orderliness, Paul seeks to regulate the process so that it contributes to the good of the whole body of Christ. Self-control, order, and concern for others must regulate the assembly while it remains open to the guidance of the Holy Spirit.

Paul's insistence that each one speak in turn prevents the kind of spiritual frenzy so common in the religious sects of Corinth (verse 27). While Paul admits that speaking in tongues can be a way of communicating with God, he insists that it be done publicly only when someone is present in the assembly to interpret its meaning in intelligible language. If an interpretation cannot be provided, the speakers should remain silent, keeping the message between themselves and God (verse 28). Likewise, Paul limits the number of prophetic utterances to two or three, and he instructs the one speaking to fall silent and listen when a new revelation comes to another (verses 29–32). He also instructs the assembly to "weigh what is said" in prophecy, discerning the significance of the messages for the church.

Paul's instructions that "women should be silent in the churches" (verse 34) seems to be in glaring contradiction to his earlier assertion that women pray and prophesy in the assembly (11:5). Moreover, plenty of evidence from Paul's other writings suggests that women played an active role in the teaching and prophesying within the churches of other cities, as seen in women like Phoebe, Prisca, Junia, Prisca, Euodia, and Syntyche. In fact, when Paul gives instructions on prophecy, he says, "You can all prophesy," an authorization that must certainly include women (verse 31). So, Paul must be referring to some other kind of speech when he says that women are not permitted "to speak." The Greek verb here means "talk" or "converse." It does not refer to proclaiming, declaring, preaching, or teaching.

Women in Greco-Roman society usually managed the domestic affairs of the household during the week while men engaged in trade and discourse in public places. So, naturally women coming to the Christian assembly on

Sundays might want to talk and visit, catching up on the news of their neighbors. Men were more accustomed to listening quietly to public speakers. In Paul's attempts to bring order to the assembly, he asked women to refrain from conversing, to be "subordinate," responsive to the needs of others.

Further, Paul says, "If there is anything they desire to know, let them ask their husbands at home" (verse 35). It seems that the women wanted to learn, especially during the biblical teachings, and were asking questions in the assembly. Since the men were more knowledgeable of the Scriptures and better educated, their wives were interrupting the prayer service with their questions. Paul recommends, then, that husbands and wives discuss these matters at home. Husbands should help their wives learn, recognizing their intellectual capacities, so they can discuss matters of faith together. Like the matter of women attending worship with their heads uncovered, the conversations and questions of women offended the cultural sensibilities of those whom Paul wanted to reach with the gospel. The focus of his words is not the silence of women but good order in Christian worship and respect for others.

In all of these instructions, Paul insists that the worship of the community reflect the character of God. If the prayer of the assembly is chaotic and conflictual, it gives the wrong impression of the God made known in Jesus Christ. This God is "a God not of disorder but of peace" (verse 33). The Corinthians, then, must learn to be at peace with one another and to express that peace in a style of worship that accentuates their complementarity and harmony.

Reflection and discussion

- In what ways does the participation of each member of my church build up the community as the body of Christ?

- What could my local church learn from Paul's instructions on communal worship and order in the assembly?

- How can I reconcile Paul's directive that "women should be silent in the churches" with his other writings that encourage women to play an active role in the teaching, prophecy, and prayer of the assembly?

- What are ways that my church can help outsiders experience the God of peace rather than feeling confused and out of place?

Prayer

God of peace, who desires to lead all people to Jesus your Son, make me more sensitive to the needs of the people around me. Encourage me to welcome others and to invite others to worship you.

SUGGESTIONS FOR FACILITATORS, GROUP SESSION 5

1. Welcome group members and ask if anyone has any questions, announcements, or requests.

2. You may want to pray this prayer as a group:
   Spirit of the Living God, who has filled the church with an abundance of gifts, help us to recognize the gifts you have given to each of us to be used for the upbuilding of the church. Unite us with a missionary desire to bring others to know Jesus Christ and to welcome others to join us in worship. Through our study of the Scriptures, give us a proper balance between the mind and the spirit, the words that encourage and challenge others, and the ability to break down divisions between us.

3. Ask one or more of the following questions:
   - What most intrigued you from this week's study?
   - What makes you want to know and understand more of God's word?

4. Discuss lessons 19 through 24. Choose one or more of the questions for reflection and discussion from each lesson to talk over as a group.

5. Ask the group members to name one thing they have most appreciated about the way the group has worked during this Bible study. Ask group members to discuss any changes they might suggest in the way the group works in future studies.

6. Invite group members to complete lessons 25 through 30 on their own during the six days before the next meeting. They should write out their own answers to the questions as preparation for next week's session.

7. Ask group members to name ways that their study of First Corinthians has helped them understand how the practices of the church are rooted in the wisdom of the cross. Discuss some of these insights.

8. Conclude by praying aloud together the prayer at the end of one of the lessons discussed. You may want to conclude the prayer by asking members to voice prayers of thanksgiving.

LESSON 25 **SESSION 6**

**I worked harder than any of them—though it was not I,
but the grace of God that is with me. Whether then it was
I or they, so we proclaim and so you have come to believe.**

1 CORINTHIANS 15:10–11

Belief in the Resurrection of Christ

1 CORINTHIANS 15:1–11 1*Now I would remind you, brothers and sisters, of the
good news that I proclaimed to you, which you in turn received, in which also you
stand,* 2*through which also you are being saved, if you hold firmly to the message
that I proclaimed to you—unless you have come to believe in vain.*

3*For I handed on to you as of first importance what I in turn had received: that
Christ died for our sins in accordance with the scriptures,* 4*and that he was buried,
and that he was raised on the third day in accordance with the scriptures,* 5*and
that he appeared to Cephas, then to the twelve.* 6*Then he appeared to more than
five hundred brothers and sisters at one time, most of whom are still alive, though
some have died. 7Then he appeared to James, then to all the apostles.* 8*Last of all,
as to one untimely born, he appeared also to me.* 9*For I am the least of the apos-
tles, unfit to be called an apostle, because I persecuted the church of God.* 10*But by
the grace of God I am what I am, and his grace toward me has not been in vain.
On the contrary, I worked harder than any of them—though it was not I, but the
grace of God that is with me.* 11*Whether then it was I or they, so we proclaim and
so you have come to believe.*

Moving from a discussion of disorderly worship to disordered belief, Paul begins a lengthy teaching on the resurrection to correct the understanding of the Corinthians. They have come to believe in life after death, but without resurrection of the dead. Paul wants the Corinthians to know that those who live in Christ and pattern their lives on his will be resurrected by God just as Christ was raised from the dead.

Paul begins by reaffirming what the Corinthians already believe—the good news of Jesus Christ taught to them by Paul (verses 1–2). They "received" this gospel in the past, they "stand" in this teaching in the present, and they are "being saved" by it in the present leading into the future. If they do not "hold firmly" to this truth and understand its implications, they jeopardize their future with God. Paul states that he "handed on" the content of the Christian faith like runners hand on a baton from one to another in a relay race (verses 3–5). The heart of the gospel, what Paul received and handed on, is this: Christ died for our sins and was buried; Christ was raised from the dead and appeared to his disciples. Paul affirms that this early creed is "of first importance." This is the essence of the Christian faith in a nutshell.

This supremely important core of belief insists that Christ died and was raised "in accordance with the scriptures." Because there are no Old Testament texts that specifically anticipate the death or resurrection of the Messiah, most probably the emphasis is on the witness of the Old Testament as a whole: God's care for creation, fidelity to the covenant, unwavering love for his people, and his power over all opposing forces. Christ's saving death and glorious resurrection was not a divine afterthought but was part and parcel of the divine plan. God's rescue of humanity from sin and death through Christ is the final phase of the story of salvation for ancient Israel.

The list of witnesses to the appearances of Christ confirms the reality of the resurrection (verses 5–7). Paul knew that the resurrection was not simply an ineffable, subjective experience or hallucination. His enumeration of a large though finite number of witnesses, noting that most were still living, indicates that there was a convincing number willing to testify that they had seen Jesus alive. Paul links his own witness to Christ's resurrection with the Lord's appearances to his original followers. These witnesses form a chain from Cephas to Paul, demonstrating the continuity of the witness that goes back to the very beginning.

Paul notes that Christ appeared to him "last of all" (verse 8). When Paul saw the risen Christ, the appearances were at an end. In this way Paul distinguishes the appearances of the risen Christ from every later type of subjective vision and personal experience of Christ. He compares his own witness to "someone untimely born." Like a fetus expelled from the womb before it was fully formed, Paul was not ready for his own new birth. The other witnesses had been able to prepare for the appearance of the risen Christ by keeping company with him during his early ministry. Paul did not. As a persecutor of the church, Paul was clearly unprepared for his own dazzling encounter with the glorious Lord (verses 9–10). Yet, God's transforming grace made him what he is for us and for Christ's church.

Reflection and discussion

- Paul urges the Corinthians to "hold firm to the message." What in my life can cause me to loosen my grip on the gospel message?

- Why does Paul emphasize that Christ appeared to him "last of all, as to one untimely born"?

Prayer

Risen Lord, who rose from the dead and appeared to Paul, make me a witness to the new life I have received in you. Give me a new appreciation of the grace that has made me what I am.

LESSON 26 SESSION 6

For if the dead are not raised, then Christ has not been raised. If Christ has not been raised, your faith is futile and you are still in your sins. 1 CORINTHIANS 15:16–17

Life's Meaning in Light of Resurrection

1 CORINTHIANS 15:12–34 *[12]Now if Christ is proclaimed as raised from the dead, how can some of you say there is no resurrection of the dead? [13]If there is no resurrection of the dead, then Christ has not been raised; [14]and if Christ has not been raised, then our proclamation has been in vain and your faith has been in vain. [15]We are even found to be misrepresenting God, because we testified of God that he raised Christ—whom he did not raise if it is true that the dead are not raised. [16]For if the dead are not raised, then Christ has not been raised. [17]If Christ has not been raised, your faith is futile and you are still in your sins. [18]Then those also who have died in Christ have perished. [19]If for this life only we have hoped in Christ, we are of all people most to be pitied.*

[20]But in fact Christ has been raised from the dead, the first fruits of those who have died. [21]For since death came through a human being, the resurrection of the dead has also come through a human being; [22]for as all die in Adam, so all will be made alive in Christ. [23]But each in his own order: Christ the first fruits, then at his coming those who belong to Christ. [24]Then comes the end, when he hands over the kingdom to God the Father, after he has destroyed every ruler and every authority and power. [25]For he must reign until he has put all his enemies under his feet. [26]The last enemy to be destroyed is death. [27]For "God has put all things in subjection under his feet." But when it says, "All things are put in subjection," it is plain that

this does not include the one who put all things in subjection under him. [28]*When*
all things are subjected to him, then the Son himself will also be subjected to the one
who put all things in subjection under him, so that God may be all in all.
[29]*Otherwise, what will those people do who receive baptism on behalf of the*
dead? If the dead are not raised at all, why are people baptized on their behalf?
[30]*And why are we putting ourselves in danger every hour?* [31]*I die every day!*
That is as certain, brothers and sisters, as my boasting of you—a boast that I make
in Christ Jesus our Lord. [32]*If with merely human hopes I fought with wild animals*
at Ephesus, what would I have gained by it? If the dead are not raised,

> *"Let us eat and drink,*
> *for tomorrow we die."*

[33]*Do not be deceived:*

> *"Bad company ruins good morals."*

[34]*Come to a sober and right mind, and sin no more; for some people have no*
knowledge of God. I say this to your shame.

Paul now states the issue that has prompted his extended discussion of the resurrection: Some of the Corinthians were saying there is no resurrection of the dead (verse 12). Apparently, some of the community believed only in continuing life after death through the survival of the soul, but not through an act of new creation by God in the resurrection of the dead. This dualistic understanding of the human person—an immortal soul imprisoned within a body that dies and corrupts—was the Greek view that dominated most of the ancient world. Paul insists that the whole human person, created by God, will be given a new, transformed bodily life through the resurrection of the dead.

He develops the argument gently and thoroughly. If there is no resurrection of the dead, then Christ cannot have been raised (verses 13, 16). And if Christ has not been raised, then the apostles have been talking empty nonsense, and those who believed them have believed empty nonsense (verses 14, 17). In which case, Christians are liars who misrepresent God (verse 15), there is no forgiveness of sins (verse 17), and those who have died as Christians are simply lost (verse 18). The Christian gospel stands or falls with the resurrection of the dead. Without the resurrection, Christianity is only a system of delusions and futile human fantasy, leaving its adherents "most to be pitied" (verse 19).

Sweeping away all the gloomy hypothetical consequences that follow from denying the resurrection, Paul triumphantly declares: "But in fact Christ has been raised from the dead" (verse 20). As a Jew, Paul had expected the resurrection to be a corporate raising of all God's people at a future time that God would determine. To claim that only Jesus was raised from the dead, before all others and before the end of the age, seems to go against the biblical expectation. Paul therefore uses the metaphor of the "first fruits," the first sheaf of the grain harvest presented at the Jewish Feast of Weeks (Pentecost) as a sign and promise of the remainder of the harvest to come. By calling the risen Christ the "first fruits of those who have died," Paul indicates that he understands the resurrection of Christ as an anticipatory promise of the general resurrection of the dead (verses 20, 23–24).

Just as Adam is a representational figure of failed humanity, the risen Christ represents renewed, resurrected humanity. Through Adam, death came into the world; through Christ will come the resurrection of the dead (verses 21–22). Paul portrays salvation as a great drama in which Christ gains victory over all the forces arrayed in opposition to God. The "last enemy" to be subdued by Christ is death itself (verses 24–26). In the resurrection of Christ, death's fate is sealed, but death is still active in creation until its final defeat. Then at the end, all who belong to Christ will be raised to life again, and Christ will hand over the kingdom to the Father so that God alone will be sovereign over all creation (verses 24, 28).

We live now in the interval between Christ's resurrection and the day of Christ's coming when the dead will be raised to life. The time of forgiveness, restoration, and victory over sin and death, promised by Israel's prophets and sages for the age to come, has already come upon the earth through the resurrection of Christ. The future age has already burst into the present age, so that we live now with a mixture of fulfillment and expectation. What happened when Christ rose from the tomb has made the world a different place and has given us the possibility to become a different kind of people.

Reflection and discussion

- What difference does it make in my present life that Jesus Christ is risen from the dead?

- What does Paul's image of the "first fruits" reveal about how Christ's resurrection relates to my own?

- What assurances do I have that death will not have the last word?

Prayer

Lord Jesus Christ, you are my hope and my life. Without you I am trapped in sin and destined for eternal death. Deepen my trust in your resurrection and in the life you have given to me.

LESSON 27 SESSION 6

Just as we have borne the image of the man of dust, we will also bear the image of the man of heaven. 1 CORINTHIANS 15:49

From Physical Body to Spiritual Body

1 CORINTHIANS 15:35–49 [35]*But someone will ask, "How are the dead raised? With what kind of body do they come?"* [36]*Fool! What you sow does not come to life unless it dies.* [37]*And as for what you sow, you do not sow the body that is to be, but a bare seed, perhaps of wheat or of some other grain.* [38]*But God gives it a body as he has chosen, and to each kind of seed its own body.* [39]*Not all flesh is alike, but there is one flesh for human beings, another for animals, another for birds, and another for fish.* [40]*There are both heavenly bodies and earthly bodies, but the glory of the heavenly is one thing, and that of the earthly is another.* [41]*There is one glory of the sun, and another glory of the moon, and another glory of the stars; indeed, star differs from star in glory.*

[42]*So it is with the resurrection of the dead. What is sown is perishable, what is raised is imperishable.* [43]*It is sown in dishonor, it is raised in glory. It is sown in weakness, it is raised in power.* [44]*It is sown a physical body, it is raised a spiritual body. If there is a physical body, there is also a spiritual body.* [45]*Thus it is written, "The first man, Adam, became a living being"; the last Adam became a life-giving spirit.* [46]*But it is not the spiritual that is first, but the physical, and then the spiritual.* [47]*The first man was from the earth, a man of dust; the second man is from heaven.* [48]*As was the man of dust, so are those who are of the dust; and as is the man of heaven, so are those who are of heaven.* [49]*Just as we have borne the image of the man of dust, we will also bear the image of the man of heaven.*

Because the earthly imagination and human language are incapable of understanding or expressing the reality of resurrection, Paul turns to metaphors and analogies to help his readers. The Corinthians naively assumed that resurrection of the dead referred to the resuscitation of the dead, physical body. They could not comprehend how an earthly embodied existence could become a heavenly embodied existence. So, Paul begins an imaginary dialogue with a generic "someone" who asks the kinds of questions raised by the Corinthians: "How are the dead raised? With what kind of body do they come?" (verse 35). In response, Paul calls his fictional dialogue partner a "fool," a term from the psalms referring to someone who fails to take the creative power of God into account. Paul then explains how resurrection entails God's transformation of the earthly body into a new and splendid state fit for the glory of eternity.

Paul first uses the image of a plant springing forth from a seed (verses 36–38). The bare seed sown in the ground first dies; then it is made alive as a growing plant. No one can predict the form of the plant from the appearance of the seed. God transforms the seed into a radically new form of existence. In the case of humans, we can see nothing in a mortal, perishing body that promises any hope of resurrection, but God will transform it through death into a body clothed with glory. With this analogy, Paul demonstrates both the radical transformation of the human body in its resurrected state and its organic continuity with the mortal body that preceded it.

Since our glorified state is indeed an embodied existence, Paul demonstrates that there are many different kinds of bodies in God's creation (verses 39–41). Each has its own distinct form, from the variety of animal life to the diverse heavenly bodies in the sky. Each body has its own kind of existence that is fitting for its environment: the earth for animals, the sky for birds, the sea for fish, and the heavens for the sun, moon, and stars. Paul uses the term "flesh" to refer to the weakness and corruptibility of earthly bodies, and the term "glory" to denote the substance of heavenly beings. As the sun, moon, and stars have a resplendence unlike anything on earth, we can expect our resurrected body, fit for a heavenly existence, to be unlike anything known on earth. The body that is raised by God will be radically changed into a glorified existence entirely different from our corruptible earthly being. Resurrection involves transformation into a new kind of body suitable for its new form of existence (verses 42–44). The body in this present life is perishable and weak; the body of those resurrected from the dead will be imperishable and glorious. What is sown on earth is a natural, physical body; what is raised is a supernatural, spiritual body.

Paul uses the representational figures of Adam and Christ to contrast humanity in its natural life and in its spiritual life to come (verses 45–49). We inherit one kind of body and life from Adam, "the man of dust," followed by a renewed, transformed body from Christ, "the man of heaven." While the present life is experienced within the parameters of space and time, enclosed within the boundaries of birth and death, the resurrection of Christ has revealed the foundation for a new eternal reality. We await the day when Christ, manifested in his resurrected body, will come from heaven to raise us and transform us into his likeness. Then, we who have borne the image of Adam will bear the image of Christ forever.

Reflection and discussion

- What are some of the main obstacles to believing in the resurrection today? How does Paul's analogy of the seed help to overcome some of these obstacles?

- How would I begin to explain the resurrected body to an unbeliever?

Prayer

Faithful God, who raised Jesus from death to eternal life, help me to trust in your promise of resurrection despite my inability to fully understand your creative power. Continue to change me day by day into the image of Christ.

Therefore, my beloved, be steadfast, immovable, always excelling in the work of the Lord, because you know that in the Lord your labor is not in vain. 1 CORINTHIANS 15:58

The Transformation of Resurrection

1 CORINTHIANS 15:50–58 50*What I am saying, brothers and sisters, is this:*
flesh and blood cannot inherit the kingdom of God, nor does the perishable inherit
the imperishable. 51*Listen, I will tell you a mystery! We will not all die, but we will*
all be changed, 52*in a moment, in the twinkling of an eye, at the last trumpet. For*
the trumpet will sound, and the dead will be raised imperishable, and we will be
changed. 53*For this perishable body must put on imperishability, and this mortal*
body must put on immortality. 54*When this perishable body puts on imperishabil-*
ity, and this mortal body puts on immortality, then the saying that is written will
be fulfilled:

"Death has been swallowed up in victory."
55*"Where, O death, is your victory?*
Where, O death, is your sting?"

56*The sting of death is sin, and the power of sin is the law.* 57*But thanks be to God,*
who gives us the victory through our Lord Jesus Christ.

58*Therefore, my beloved, be steadfast, immovable, always excelling in the work*
of the Lord, because you know that in the Lord your labor is not in vain.

Concluding his discourse on the resurrection, Paul agrees with the Corinthians who state that the physical, earthly body—"flesh and blood"—is unfit to receive eternal life—"the kingdom of God" (verse 50). In terms more compatible with the Greek mindset, "the perishable" is unsuited to become "the imperishable." But the implication drawn by the Corinthians—that resurrection from the dead is unachievable—is wrong.

So, Paul continues to teach by disclosing the "mystery," which reveals how the seemingly impossible will happen (verse 51). "Mystery," in Paul's writings, refers to a truth that was formerly hidden and undiscoverable by human reason alone but has now been divinely revealed. Christ will come in glory, and he will transform us into his likeness. This will happen "in a moment, in the twinkling of an eye, at the last trumpet"—all attempts to express the divine, wondrous, ineffable nature of the transforming event. On that day "we will all be changed," both the dead and those still alive. This dramatic transformation, as our perishable, mortal bodies will put on imperishability and immortality, will be accomplished by God's creative power (verses 53–54).

Paul describes this mystery of transformation with a clothing imagery. The transformation to an immortal body is accomplished by adding a new garment to the mortal body. We do not have to slip off our earthly body before being garbed in the heavenly one. Like the seed that dies and becomes the full plant, the mortal body is radically changed into the risen body in glory. Thus, we know that God does not plan to destroy our bodies and start again but to transform our bodies, not to reject his creation but to redeem it. The baptismal garment reflects this idea of putting on the risen life of Christ.

Although our final transformation is anticipated for the future, we already begin to experience this eternal life in the present when we live in Christ. God's ultimate victory over death is now assured, so we can even today sing a taunting victory song over the fallen enemy: "Where, O death, is your victory? Where, O death, is your sting?" (verse 55). Death's stinging power to evoke fear, depression, and despair is already defeated through Christ. The sting of death is provided by our sin, and sin is spurred on by the law, but Christ has forgiven our sins, redeemed us from the law, and risen from the dead. He has delivered the world from the tyranny of sin, law, and death. He has absorbed death's venom and drained its potency so that victory now belongs to God's people. We can now sneer defiantly at death's impotence before the saving power and forgiving mercy of God.

Paul's teaching gives way to thanksgiving to God for giving "the victory through our Lord Jesus Christ" (verse 57). This present victory is a triumph that all God's people can share now. Paul's praise then leads to a three-part exhortation to his readers, his beloved (verse 58). First, Paul urges us to "be steadfast, immovable," holding firmly to the foundational truth of Christ's death and resurrection. Second, he insists that we be "always excelling in the work of the Lord," contributing to building up the church. Third, he exhorts us to know that in the Lord our labor is "not in vain." Although our work for Christ may lead us into life-threatening peril, God will use it to bring growth to the church and reward to the laborer. Although our present life is under the cross, it is sustained by hope in the resurrection.

Reflection and discussion

- What is the mystery of God that Paul reveals? How does it change everything?

- In what way does the baptismal garment express the transformation a person experiences in Christ?

- In what ways do Paul's final words (verse 58) give purpose and meaning to the life I live each day?

- Why do people sometimes fear death? In what ways do Paul's words take away the sting of death for me?

- What has most inspired me from Paul's teaching on resurrection in chapter 15?

Prayer

Lord Jesus Christ, you have won victory for the world over the powers of sin and death. Thank you for giving me hope and confidence in the future. Help me live a life that is worth living for eternity.

I do not want to see you now just in passing, for I hope to spend some time with you, if the Lord permits.

1 CORINTHIANS 16:7

Paul's Travel Itineraries

1 CORINTHIANS 16:1–12 *1 Now concerning the collection for the saints: you should follow the directions I gave to the churches of Galatia. 2 On the first day of every week, each of you is to put aside and save whatever extra you earn, so that collections need not be taken when I come. 3 And when I arrive, I will send any whom you approve with letters to take your gift to Jerusalem. 4 If it seems advisable that I should go also, they will accompany me.*

5 I will visit you after passing through Macedonia—for I intend to pass through Macedonia—6 and perhaps I will stay with you or even spend the winter, so that you may send me on my way, wherever I go. 7 I do not want to see you now just in passing, for I hope to spend some time with you, if the Lord permits. 8 But I will stay in Ephesus until Pentecost, 9 for a wide door for effective work has opened to me, and there are many adversaries.

10 If Timothy comes, see that he has nothing to fear among you, for he is doing the work of the Lord just as I am; 11 therefore let no one despise him. Send him on his way in peace, so that he may come to me; for I am expecting him with the brothers.

12 Now concerning our brother Apollos, I strongly urged him to visit you with the other brothers, but he was not at all willing to come now. He will come when he has the opportunity.

Before closing his letter, Paul responds to one more question asked by the Corinthians in their letter to him: "concerning the collection for the saints" (verses 1–2). His directions pertain only to gathering and delivering this monetary offering. Presumably the Christians of Corinth already know the purpose of this project from Paul's previous communication. From his letters to other communities, we know that he was gathering a large collection from among his Gentile congregations to be given to the poor among the Jewish Christians in Jerusalem (Rom 15:25–31). He envisioned this collection as a sign of unity between Gentiles and Jews in Christ and as an expression of gratitude from the Gentiles throughout the world for the spiritual blessings given to them by the mother church in Jerusalem.

Here Paul instructs the Corinthians to set aside any surplus income they earn each week and save it for the time of his arrival. Rather than target wealthy donors, he calls on everyone to participate according to their ability so that the gift will represent the whole community. By asking the Corinthians to collect the money in their weekly gatherings on the Lord's Day, he avoids the need to launch a fund-raising drive when he arrives. In Jewish culture, generosity toward the poor flowed from compassion for their plight and obedience to God's commands, whereas in Greco-Roman society charity was offered to bring honor to oneself and social prestige. Paul's method for collecting funds shows his concern that the Corinthians be generous to people they have never met in order to give honor to God and not themselves. He hopes that the gift will alleviate the suffering in Jerusalem and express the reality that in Christ there is neither Jew nor Greek.

In order to assure the Corinthians that the funds represent their own community, Paul asks them to choose their own delegates to personally deliver the funds to Jerusalem (verses 3–4). This personal representation from the Gentile communities enhances the symbolic value of this gesture of unity. Paul has developed a strategy whereby Gentile converts from across the world will come face-to-face with Jewish Christians in the mother church. Paul will send letters of introduction with the delegates, or if it seems advisable, he will lead them personally to Jerusalem.

Before returning to Corinth, Paul has other plans (verses 5–9). Presently he intends to stay in Ephesus—from where he is writing this letter—until Pentecost, the Jewish feast occurring on the fiftieth day after Passover. In this important city, Paul is facing both opportunities and opposition. The "wide door for effective work" refers to promising conditions for preaching the gospel, despite the presence of adversaries there. Later, while the weather is still favorable for travel, he will pass through Macedonia and then to Corinth. He will stay with them for an extended period, perhaps offering needed correction and counsel during his visit. Of course, all of his plans are qualified with an important stipulation: "if the Lord permits," meaning that God directs his paths.

Meanwhile, Paul has sent Timothy to continue "the work of the Lord" and to remind the Corinthians of Paul's "ways in Christ Jesus" (verses 10–11; 4:17). Paul seems concerned about the treatment Timothy will receive from the Corinthians, for he counsels them to provide the conditions so that "he has nothing to fear" among them, and he warns them not to "despise him." By sending this letter, which calls for basic changes in the behavior of the Corinthians, Paul may be increasing the tension between himself and the community. Since Timothy comes as Paul's surrogate, attacking Timothy would be the best way to demonstrate displeasure at Paul. The Corinthians may also be disappointed that Timothy is visiting them rather than Apollos (verse 12). Although Paul had urged Apollos to return to Corinth, he doesn't tell us the reason why Apollos was unwilling to travel at the present time. Paul only hopes that Timothy will accomplish his mission in the community and that they will "send him on his way in peace" to return to Paul along with "the brothers" who are delivering this letter to the Corinthians.

Reflection and discussion

- What might "the collection for the saints" teach the Christians in both Corinth and Jerusalem?

- What does Paul's method for the collection teach me about how to give alms for those in need?

- In what way is Paul's collection for the church in Jerusalem a tangible expression of the truths he has been teaching throughout this letter?

- Paul saw both opportunity and risk in Ephesus. What areas of mission today offer much opposition but also wide openings for evangelization?

Prayer

Risen Lord, who has united Jews and Gentiles as one, bring unity to your church through an ecumenism of compassion. Help me to reach out to those in need with generosity so that you may be honored and not myself.

LESSON 30 SESSION 6

All the brothers and sisters send greetings.
Greet one another with a holy kiss.
1 CORINTHIANS 16:20

Final Messages and Greetings

1 CORINTHIANS 16:13–24 [13]*Keep alert, stand firm in your faith, be courageous, be strong.* [14]*Let all that you do be done in love.*

[15]*Now, brothers and sisters, you know that members of the household of Stephanas were the first converts in Achaia, and they have devoted themselves to the service of the saints;* [16]*I urge you to put yourselves at the service of such people, and of everyone who works and toils with them.* [17]*I rejoice at the coming of Stephanas and Fortunatus and Achaicus, because they have made up for your absence;* [18]*for they refreshed my spirit as well as yours. So give recognition to such persons.*

[19]*The churches of Asia send greetings. Aquila and Prisca, together with the church in their house, greet you warmly in the Lord.* [20]*All the brothers and sisters send greetings. Greet one another with a holy kiss.*

[21]*I, Paul, write this greeting with my own hand.* [22]*Let anyone be accursed who has no love for the Lord. Our Lord, come!* [23]*The grace of the Lord Jesus be with you.* [24]*My love be with all of you in Christ Jesus.*

A series of imperatives marks the conclusion of Paul's letter (verses 13–14). The first exhorts the community to "keep alert," waiting intently for the coming of the Lord and behaving in a way appropriate to that hope. The second urges them to "stand firm" in their faith, remaining fixed in the teachings Paul passed on to them concerning the death and resurrection of Christ. Next, Paul insists that the community "be courageous" and "be strong" in the face of the extraordinary pressures exerted by the pagan society in which they live. And finally, he encourages them with the words, "Let all that you do be done in love," reiterating his emphasis on Christian love that runs throughout the letter. Such love will direct their spiritual gifts to the service of Christ's body, guide their decisions about food offered to idols, shepherd their treatment of the needy at the Lord's Supper, and heal the wounds created by their lawsuits and divisions.

Offering an example of what love in action looks like, Paul praises the members of the household of Stephanas, for they have "devoted themselves to the service of the saints" (verse 15). These were the "first converts" (literally, *the first fruits*) in Achaia and among the few Corinthians baptized by Paul (1:16). Stephanas, along with two companions, Fortunatus and Achaicus, came to Paul in Ephesus, delivering the letter from the Corinthian church and providing further information to Paul about the community there (verse 17).

Most probably, these three are also to be the bearers of Paul's present letter to the Corinthians. They will present this letter to the community, verify its content, deliver oral messages from Paul, be present when the letter is read in the assembly on the Lord's Day, and respond to any questions that arise after its reading. So, Paul urges his readers to give them "recognition" and put themselves in their "service."

Paul sends greetings from the churches of Asia, those communities of Christians that include Ephesus and surrounding cities (verse 19). He adds the personal greetings of Aquila and Prisca, a husband and wife missionary team that Paul first met in Corinth, who are now with him in Ephesus. The "brothers and sisters" are all the members of the churches, belonging to a new supernatural family in Christ. Paul urges them to express their familial intimacy by greeting one another with a "holy kiss" (verse 20). This sign of Christian unity and love would later become a formalized part of the church's eucharistic liturgy. Here the holy kiss expresses the joy, reconciliation, and peace that all believers share in Christ, whether they are Jew or Gentile, Greek or Roman, slave or free, woman or man.

Because the letter has been dictated by Paul to a secretary, Paul takes up a pen to sign the letter. With his signature, he writes a final note with his own hand (verses 21–24). His invocation, "Our Lord, come!" is in Aramaic (*Maranatha*). It can mean "Our Lord has come!", "Our Lord is coming!", "Our Lord is now present!" (all declarations of faith), or "Our Lord, come!" (a plea for Christ to come in glory). It is most probably a liturgical acclamation, offering a curse to those without love, and blessings for those who experience the grace of the Lord Jesus.

Reflection and discussion

- What specific action could I take in order to follow each of Paul's exhortations in verses 13–14?

- What questions might the assembly in Corinth have asked of Stephanas after Paul's letter was read to them?

- Why is the *Maranatha* acclamation particularly expressive of the Lord's coming in the Christian Eucharist?

Prayer

God our Father, through the grace of our Lord Jesus Christ and the inspiration of the Holy Spirit, you have given Paul's letter to the church. Help me to accept the challenges it offers me and to become a more intimate member of your family.

SUGGESTIONS FOR FACILITATORS, GROUP SESSION 6

1. Welcome group members and make any final announcements or requests.

2. You may want to pray this prayer as a group:
   Faithful God, who sent your Son Jesus Christ to take up the cross and to rise in glory to give us life, help us to understand the challenges you offer to us through the writings of Paul. Deepen our gratitude for all you have given us as members of the body of Christ. Keep us alert, firm in faith, strong and courageous, and always excelling in the work of the Lord. Give us confidence in the future so that our labor is not in vain, and may everything we do be done in love.

3. Ask one or more of the following questions:
   - How has this study of First Corinthians enriched your life?
   - In what way has this study challenged you the most?

4. Discuss lessons 25 through 30. Choose one or more of the questions for reflection and discussion from each lesson to discuss as a group.

5. Ask the group if they would like to study another in the *Threshold Bible Study* series. Discuss the topic and dates, and make a decision among those interested. Ask the group members to suggest people they would like to invite to participate in the next study series.

6. Ask the group to discuss the insights that stand out most from this study over the past six weeks.

7. Conclude by praying aloud the following prayer or another of your own choosing:
   Holy Spirit of the living God, you inspired the writers of the Scriptures and you have guided our study during these weeks. Continue to deepen our love for the word of God in the holy Scriptures, and draw us more deeply into the heart of Jesus. We thank you for the confident hope you have placed within us and the gifts that build up the church. Through this study, lead us to worship and witness more fully and fervently, and bless us now and always with the fire of your love.